BABY&
TODDLER
MEALS

Also by Robin Barker
Baby Love
The Mighty Toddler

ROBIN BARKER

BABY & TODDLER MEALS

MACMILLAN

Pan Macmillan Australia

NOTE TO READERS

All care has been taken to provide accurate, safe information but it is impossible to cover every situation, so please consult a competent health professional whenever you are in doubt about your baby's health or behaviour. A book can never be a substitute for an individual professional consultation. The author and the publishers cannot accept legal responsibility for any problems arising out of the contents of this book.

First published 1998 in Macmillan by Pan Macmillan Australia Pty Limited
This edition published 2004 in Macmillan by Pan Macmillan Australia Pty Limited
1 Market St, Sydney

Reprinted 2005, 2006, 2007 (twice)

National Library of Australia
cataloguing-in-publication data:

Barker, Robin, 1944– .
Baby and toddler meals.

ISBN 978 1 4050 3635 1

1. Cookery (Baby foods). 2. Baby foods. 3. Infants – Nutrition. I. Title.

641.5622

Design by Deborah Parry Graphics
Typeset in Centaur 13.5/16pt by Post Pre-press Group
Produced in Australia by Mcpherson's Printing Group

Papers used by Pan Macmillan Australia Pty Ltd are natural, recyclable products made from wood grown in sustainable forests. The manufacturing processes conform to the environmental regulations of the country of origin.

For my mother, Dot Roche, one of that extraordinary generation of women who cooked great food for her family three times a day, seven days a week, twelve months of the year.

He, she and so on
Once again the baby and toddler in this book seem to be 'she' . . .
next time I promise it will be 'he'.

Acknowledgements

What fun I have had revisiting the baby and toddler food years.

I am very grateful to Jann Zintgraff and Margaret O'Sullivan for their expertise so generously given to help build and cook the recipes.

The Zintgraff kitchen is to be revered. Roger and I are fortunate indeed to share many magnificent meals with Jann and Alain and friends. Thank you, Jann, for being such a wonderful friend and cook.

Margaret O'Sullivan is not only my agent but also the author of many excellent cookbooks. Another committed 'foodie' who helped test and taste. Thank you, Margaret.

The idea was Jane Curry's, publisher at Pan Macmillan. Jane's enthusiasm for the book kept me moving along when I started to get bogged down in mashed banana and avocado.

Many friends and families gave me ideas and recipes and tested dishes. A big thank you to you all.

Contents

Introduction

Feeding babies and toddlers is an area of great interest to parents and in the last twenty years there has been an explosion of information about infant nutrition. Good information is generally easily available, but I am aware from my work that it is also an area of baby care that causes quite a lot of worry, which is unfortunate.

I think the main reasons for this are conflicting advice, lack of flexible guidelines, fear of terrible consequences if rules are broken, overreaction to the possibility of allergies and not enough allowance made for the wide range of variations in baby behaviour in response to eating. I sometimes see feeding charts for babies in their first year that are so complicated they nearly make me faint dead away, so it's no wonder parents stress out at times. The aim of this book is to give you safe, simple and flexible guidelines and a bunch of recipes to try – some for babies only, but most are family food that babies and toddlers can share.

A vital part of feeding babies is being aware of the wide variations in behaviour that they exhibit across the eating spectrum, so I have described as many of these as I can think of – you might find one that fits your baby exactly.

I have included some basics of nutrition somewhat reluctantly, as I am aware how parents agonise over the five food groups and the possibility of their babies and toddlers suffering from nutritional deficiencies. To offset that, I have covered as many potential problem areas as possible to allay anxieties about the possibilities of malnutrition!

Food is a most enjoyable part of life and you will find it is exciting helping your baby on the journey. You might also find it messy and perhaps frustrating, but stay cool and, above all, keep smiling.

PART ONE

GETTING STARTED

CHAPTER 1

General Guidelines for Feeding Your Baby and Toddler

Build up to a Variety of Foods

Babies and toddlers often have periods where they are very selective about what they will and won't eat, but offering them a variety of foods makes it much less likely that they will consume excessive or inadequate amounts of any one food.

Limit 'Bad' Fat. Offer a Moderate Amount of 'Good' Fat

Between birth and age 2, fat is needed as a concentrated source of energy, and for brain development. Fifty per cent of a baby's energy intake should come from fat during these years. This should decrease to about 30 per cent between the ages of 2 and 5.

There is now strong evidence to suggest that from age 2, high cholesterol levels in children's blood tend to stay high, increasing the risk of heart disease in middle or late adult life. Consequently, the recommendations for toddlers' and pre-schoolers' dietary fat have changed to the following.

Birth to 2 years

During the first year use breastmilk and/or infant formula and, after solids are introduced at 6 months, full-fat dairy products in meals. During the second year continue with breastmilk and/or full-fat milk as the main drink and full-fat dairy products. Ideally, give the milk from a cup instead of a bottle.

A note about soy formula and soy liquid: Whole cow's milk is preferable to soy liquid as it contains naturally occurring ingredients necessary for good nutrition (for example, fat, calcium and iron) that are not present in unfortified soy drink. It is now recommended that soy drink not be used until after age 2.

It's not a good idea to use either soy formula or drink indiscriminately as there are growing concerns, especially for the first two years, about possible nutritional and other problems related to soy. These include the presence of plant hormones known as phytoestrogens, the high levels of aluminium in soy formula and the lack of the naturally occurring ingredients mentioned above. Some research has also shown a higher incidence of infections in babies fed soy formula than in babies fed cow's milk formula.

There are very few cases where soy formula is required in the first year as there is now a range of cow's milk formula designed to accommodate lactose or cow's milk protein intolerance. Soy drink does not have to be used as a substitute for healthy toddlers who won't drink milk. Water is fine as a drink, and dairy products can be included in their diets.

2 to 5 years

From age 2 reduced-fat dairy foods and drinks can be commenced (advisable for the whole family). Skim milk should not be used for this age group. As much as possible, use 'good fat' (low saturated fat) foods and avoid 'bad fat' (high saturated fat) foods.

From 5 years

The general healthy dietary guidelines recommended for adults — that is, a diet moderate in total fat and low in saturated fat — are appropriate for children 5 years and over. Skim milk and skim milk products are fine in this age group.

Examples of good fats (eat in moderate amounts)

Breastmilk, fish, oils (olive, canola, sesame, corn, peanut), wheatgerm, avocado, chicken (skin removed), lean meat and pork.

Examples of bad fats — the stuff we all love (a small amount is okay)

Full-cream dairy products, fried food, fatty meat, fatty bacon, crisps, biscuits, pastries, cakes, donuts.

For children, avoid diets low in *total* fat

Confusing, isn't it? Occasionally, because parents take the above guidelines to extremes and/or because of genetic cholesterol problems, children are put on low-fat diets that may cause failure to thrive, chronic diarrhoea and even delayed development. Diets low in total fat are potentially hazardous for babies, toddlers and children, and if necessary for medical reasons need supervision and monitoring by a suitable health professional, such as a paediatrician or dietitian.

Provide Plenty of Fruit, Vegetables (including lentils) and Grains

These foods provide essential nutrients such as vitamins A and C, as well as carbohydrates, fibre and essential minerals, and are an excellent way to diversify your baby's diet. Combinations of these foods provide good family meals that babies and toddlers can share and are excellent as finger foods and snacks.

Provide Only a Small Amount of Sugar and Food Containing Added Sugars

Excessive sugar in babies' and toddlers' diets can cause problems such as black teeth, diarrhoea and a reduction in their appetite for nutritious food. Inappropriate use of sugar also interferes with establishing good eating habits in childhood. One of the most common ways toddlers get too much sugar is from fruit juice. Water is the best drink for extra fluids. One juice a day is plenty. Try to give it in a cup instead of a bottle.

However, judicious use of sugar as a small part of a balanced diet is acceptable. A little sugar helps with constipation, acts as a preserving agent, and adds moisture and flavour to many foods.

Choose Foods that are Low in Salt. Avoid Adding Salt to Foods Prepared for Babies Under 12 Months

Sodium intake should be low in the first year of life as babies have a limited capacity to excrete excessive sodium, which may cause kidney damage. After the first year it is best to limit salty foods, as it is in the early childhood years that the taste for salt is set and there is now a proven link between salt intake and high blood pressure in adults. Freshly cooked family meals that have a pinch of salt added for culinary purposes are not the problem. Excessive salt intake is more related to manufactured food, processed food, fast food and takeaway food: a high intake of these foods should be avoided, not just for toddlers but for the whole family.

Provide Foods Containing Iron and Calcium

Babies and toddlers need to be offered foods that supply good sources of iron and calcium (see pages 11–12). These minerals are important for healthy blood, proper growth and strong bones.

Your Baby's Nutritional Requirements

Here are the five essential nutrients your baby needs for health and growth once breastmilk or formula is not meeting her total nutritional needs. (This gradually starts to happen between 6 and 12 months of age.)

Remember that many combinations of different foods can supply all five nutrients, which is why diets can vary considerably and still be healthy.

1. Carbohydrates (complex, sugars and dietary fibre)

Carbohydrates provide fuel, energy and fibre.

EXAMPLES OF COMPLEX CARBOHYDRATES (INCLUDES NATURAL AND REFINED)

Bananas, spinach, flour (white and wholemeal), rolled oats, potatoes, bread (white and wholemeal), avocado, carrots, pasta, baked beans.

EXAMPLES OF SUGARS (INCLUDES NATURAL AND REFINED)

Natural sultanas, dates, dried apricots, bananas, white grapes, apples, oranges. Refined sugar, honey, golden syrup, jam, sweet biscuits.

EXAMPLES OF DIETARY FIBRE

Vegetables, fruit, cereal, fruit juice.

2. Protein

Protein is needed for growth and repair of body cells. Small children need much more protein for their size than adults do. In general, if children are offered a variety of foods from the five food groups they are unlikely to be deficient in protein. Care needs to be taken with vegetarian diets, especially vegan diets, which exclude dairy products (see Chapter 2).

EXAMPLES OF ANIMAL PROTEIN

Milk, cheese, eggs, fish, chicken, meat, yoghurt, liver, brains, kidneys.

EXAMPLES OF PLANT PROTEIN

Plant proteins need to be combined to provide nourishment for proper growth. In the right combinations they are as useful as animal proteins: brown rice, cooked pasta, cooked lentils, bread, flour, breakfast cereals, wheatgerm, cooked haricot beans, dates.

3. Vitamins

Vitamins are needed in tiny amounts in the body to help absorb other nutrients or to speed up chemical reactions. The body cannot produce them, so they must be supplied by food. Vitamins are classified as fat-soluble (A, D, E and K) or water-soluble (the B group and C). Fat-soluble vitamins are found in the food fats and are fairly stable. Water-soluble vitamins are found in vegetables, grains, meat and milk, and are sensitive to heat and over-exposure.

THE QUESTION OF VITAMIN SUPPLEMENTS

Breastfed babies do not need vitamin supplements. Breastmilk is a good source of all vitamins. Formula-fed babies do not need vitamin supplements, as all the necessary vitamins are added. (Look on the side of the tin.)

Premature babies, whether breastfed or formula-fed, need

extra supplements for the first three to four months after birth as they don't arrive with stores of vitamins.

Healthy non-eating toddlers being offered a wide variety of food do not need supplements. Occasionally, vitamin supplements may have a place for babies or toddlers who have serious medical conditions. Toddlers having a vegan diet (see Chapter 2) need a vitamin B12 supplement, as vitamin B12 is only found in animal foods. Generally, vitamin supplements are unnecessary and a waste of money.

4. Minerals

Minerals are important for healthy blood, proper growth and strong bones. Like vitamins, minerals have to be provided by the diet. Eating a variety of foods ensures that your body gets all the minerals it needs. The important ones for babies and toddlers are iron and calcium.

IRON

Iron is needed for healthy blood and muscles. There is concern that iron deficiency is a problem for some groups of babies and toddlers.

Foods that Supply Iron

Breastmilk, infant formula, lean meat, liver, kidneys, beans, peas and lentils, dark green vegetables, iron-fortified cereals (check labels), dried apricots, dates, wholegrain cereals and pasta.

The Question of Iron Supplements

Iron supplements are needed for premature babies for three to four months after birth as they don't arrive with sufficient iron stores.

Some evidence exists that exclusively breastfed babies who are eating very little food in the second six months (a normal variation – see page 43) need an iron supplement. Unfortunately, when these babies are obviously thriving and look well, the only way to know if they are iron deficient is to take a blood test.

Because opinion is still divided about the age at which breastmilk alone does not supply adequate iron, I am very reluctant to suggest blood tests and supplements routinely for thriving, exclusively breastfed babies in the second six months. If you are concerned, talk to your family doctor or paediatrician.

Healthy non-eating toddlers being offered a wide variety of food do not need iron supplements; however, it's a good idea not to allow them to drink unlimited quantities of cow's milk from bottles. Large amounts of cow's milk and no food does lead to iron deficiency in some toddlers.

Toddlers on a vegan diet (see Chapter 2) may need an iron supplement.

Once your baby is eating a variety of foods, serving some food containing vitamin C with as many meals as possible can enhance iron absorption. Vitamin C is found in fresh fruit and vegetables.

CALCIUM
Calcium is needed for good bone growth and strong teeth.

Foods that Supply Calcium
Milk and dairy products such as cheese and yoghurt are the best sources of calcium and most easily absorbed by the body.

Calcium is also found in the following foods, but in much less quantity than in milk or dairy products:

- Tofu.
- Canned fish with bones.
- Some fruit and vegetables – broccoli, brussels sprouts, oranges and pulses. (Baked beans are quite a good source of calcium.)

- Nuts and seeds – almonds, sesame seeds and tahini. (Whole nuts should never be given to children, and because of the possibility of an allergic response, ground nuts should be avoided until after the first year.)

5. Water

Water is a vital nutrient. Breastmilk has plenty of water in it, so well-nourished breastfed babies do not need extra water, even in hot weather. Formula also has plenty of water. Formula-fed babies only need water as well as their formula if they are constipated (hard poo).

Once babies are eating a variety of food, water can be offered at various times throughout the day if you think your baby needs it. It is an excellent idea to encourage the use of water as an extra fluid, rather than fruit juice, for the following reasons:

- Water is usually self-limiting (the toddler only drinks to relieve thirst) and so it doesn't interfere with appetite for other foods.
- Juice (and soft drink and cordial) is a common cause of diarrhoea if consumed in large amounts.
- Large amounts of juice are a major contributor to tooth decay and erosion. Fruit juice is useful for constipation and as a source of vitamin C for older babies and toddlers, but one drink of juice a day is sufficient.

CHAPTER 2

Some Other Important Bits and Pieces

Cholesterol

Cholesterol is a fat found in blood. It is used by the body to make certain hormones, as well as nerve and brain cells. Most blood cholesterol is made within the body from foods containing saturated fats or cholesterol. High levels of blood cholesterol can cause fatty plaques to form on the walls of blood vessels. In adult life, these blood vessels can break down or develop clots on their surface and eventually block off arteries, causing serious disability or death.

Foods high in saturated fats — for example, deep-fried food and fatty meat — are the main culprits for raising blood cholesterol. Foods that actually contain cholesterol — for example, eggs and prawns — don't play a major role, so it is fine to give your toddler an egg a day if she likes them (and is not allergic to them).

Vegetarian Diets for Babies and Toddlers

Many families now choose not to eat meat. It is relatively easy to provide adequate nutrients for toddlers from a vegetarian diet that includes dairy products (with or without eggs).

Vegetarian diets that do not include any animal products (vegan diets), however, pose problems for babies and toddlers as these diets tend to be bulky and offer a limited range of food, which little people with fussy appetites are likely to have problems with.

A continuing shortage of protein, vitamin B12, iron, calcium and fat in vegan diets, as well as an overall shortage of calories, can put a baby or toddler's growth at risk.

Some of the problems can be overcome by continuing breastfeeding and/or the use of a soy infant formula, mixing liberal amounts of smooth peanut butter (not until over 1 year, and may be problematic for toddlers with eczema or food allergies) and tahini (sesame seed paste; also a potential problem for toddlers with allergies) into dishes before serving and giving a vitamin B12 and iron supplement.

What is an Allergy?

An allergy is an overreaction of the body's immune system to a foreign antibody, usually a protein. Allergic reactions are often caused by food proteins but may also be caused by proteins in medication, chemicals, dust, smoke, insect bites, pet hair, pollutants or dust mite poo. Allergic reactions may be immediate, within two hours, or delayed, happening up to 48 hours after eating the food. Immediate reactions are more likely to be due to food allergy, delayed reactions to food intolerance.

Some food allergy facts

- The number of children experiencing allergic reactions to food is rising in Western society. About 4–6 per cent of babies, toddlers and preschoolers now have a true food allergy – egg, milk and peanut protein being the most common. Other foods include the protein in wheat, fish, soybeans, nuts, sesame seeds and berries.

- Allergy and intolerance to food is more common in young children because their immune system is not fully developed. Most children grow out of their allergies before starting school – less than 1 per cent of adults have food allergies, usually to peanuts, tree nuts and fish.

- No one is too sure why there is an increase in food allergies, but it is unlikely that it is due to food additives. Some experts think it is because young children are exposed to a much greater range of foods than previous generations were. Others think it may be because modern living and medicines have so dramatically decreased the number of infections in early childhood that, instead of fighting off bacteria and viruses, babies' immune systems are now fighting off food proteins.

- Food allergy is often inherited. Toddlers who have one family member with asthma or eczema have a 20–40 per cent higher risk of developing a food allergy. If there are two or more family members with allergies the risk increases to 50–80 per cent.

Allergic reactions
NON LIFE-THREATENING REACTIONS
Reactions may be immediate (two hours or less), or delayed (up to 48 hours) after the food is ingested. Common allergic symptoms include swelling around the eyes and mouth, flushing of the skin, rashes and hives. Other symptoms include excessive mucous, abdominal cramps, diarrhoea and vomiting.

LIFE-THREATENING REACTIONS
A small number of toddlers experience life-threatening reactions

to food, peanuts and egg being the most common allergens. This is called anaphylactic shock.

ANAPHYLACTIC SHOCK

Signs and Symptoms of Anaphylactic Shock – Rapid Onset

- noisy/difficult breathing, wheeziness
- swelling of throat and tongue
- hoarse voice
- paleness, floppiness
- loss of consciousness

In some cases, anaphylaxis is preceded by the non life-threatening reactions described on page 16. Most babies/toddlers who experience the lesser reaction to food do not go on to have a life-threatening event, but a small number do, some-times the next time the food is introduced.

Steps to Follow for Unexpected Anaphylactic Shock (when there is no adrenalin in the home)

1. Dial 000. State that a toddler is having an *anaphylactic reaction* and requires rapid transport to hospital via an *intensive care ambulance.* Give full address, phone number and postcode.

2. Lie the toddler flat and raise her feet (if possible).

3. Remove the food from her mouth.

4. If she stops breathing, commence heart–lung resuscitation.

Note: Be prepared. Heart–lung resuscitation courses are available in your state from the Royal Lifesaving Society, the Red Cross and St John's Ambulance. Single-page charts of basic resuscitation techniques are available from children's hospitals in all states. Pin one on the back of the toilet door where you will have a constant reminder of what to do.

TRACKING DOWN THE ALLERGEN IN NON LIFE-THREATENING REACTIONS

It can be difficult to work out if a rash, runny nose or swelling around the mouth is due to food or a viral infection. During their first three years, when babies and toddlers are being introduced to food, many have mild reactions that are not serious. It's simply a matter of waiting a month or two and trying again.

Toddlers who react to peanuts have a higher chance of reacting to egg, milk or soy as well, although not always. As allergies develop over time, the reaction may not occur until a toddler has eaten the food a few times. And sometimes the food is fine in one form but not in another – for example, yoghurt may be tolerated when milk is not.

Laboratory tests are unreliable in diagnosing allergic reactions, although a skin prick test can be a guide. Sometimes the results of laboratory tests are used to inappropriately restrict diets in ways that may not protect against the allergy and may put the toddler's nutritional status at risk. Alternative tests such as hair and saliva testing and kinesiology are of no use – save your money.

The most reliable way to test for food allergy remains excluding the food for a set period, then reintroducing it – this is known as a food challenge. A food challenge may be done on its own or in conjunction with a laboratory test.

A food challenge is not as simple as it sounds, because milk, egg or peanut proteins are found in many foods. Guidance from a dietitian, paediatrician or allergy specialist is advisable to find out exactly what foods should be avoided and what substitutes should be used in order to ensure a nutritionally adequate diet.

TRACKING DOWN THE ALLERGEN IN LIFE-THREATENING REACTIONS

Identifying the cause of anaphylaxis is obviously very important. Often it appears to be self-evident (coincides with eating a peanut butter sandwich or an egg); nevertheless, you will need to discuss it in detail with your doctor to exclude other conditions that can be confused with anaphylaxis. This may be followed by allergy testing (blood or skin prick) to help confirm or exclude *all* potential triggers.

Long-term management includes referral to an allergy specialist, education on the avoidance of the trigger(s), which will include advice from a paediatric allergy dietitian, and provision of an Anaphylaxis Action Plan.

MINIMISING THE RISKS OF LIFE-THREATENING ALLERGIC REACTIONS TO FOOD: GENERAL GUIDELINES FOR BABIES AND TODDLERS

Although the number of babies and toddlers experiencing anaphylaxis triggered by food allergy is increasing statistically, the numbers remain small. Most babies and toddlers tolerate a wide range of foods without disastrous consequences.

Because it is nutritionally advantageous for older babies and toddlers to be offered a varied diet, it is not advisable to strictly limit the diet of the general population because of the small possibility of a severe reaction. A life-threatening reaction to food (or medication, bee sting or anything else) is a frightening event for parents. However, there has to be a balance between protecting vulnerable children while still ensuring that the vast majority of babies and toddlers do not have their diets unnecessarily restricted — which can lead to its own problems.

Research is currently being undertaken with the aim of accurately documenting the incidence and cause of life-threatening reactions to food, to help determine appropriate management strategies for allergic babies, toddlers and children. Until we have guidelines arising out of that research, *the following is recommended if your baby or toddler has eczema, asthma or a family history of allergies:*

- Breastfeed as long as possible. Breastfeeding delays the onset and reduces the severity of allergies.
- Introduce solids after age 6 months. Start with foods least likely to cause allergic reactions — rice cereal, apple, pear, carrot, potato. Take your time introducing new foods, so that if your baby has a reaction you can work out what it is from.
- Avoid using products that contain nut oil — for example, almond oil — on the skin.
- If you are breastfeeding, do not eat peanut or tree nut products.
- Avoid giving your baby/toddler peanut products indefinitely.
- Avoid giving your baby cow's milk, soy, eggs, fish, strawberries and sesame products until after a year. If in doubt, seek advice about the best time to introduce these foods from a paediatric dietitian or allergy specialist.
- Do not hesitate to get medical advice/help immediately if your baby/toddler has a sudden, severe reaction to food (wheezing, breathing difficulties, sudden voluminous vomiting or facial swelling).

What is Food Intolerance?

Food intolerance is more common than food allergy. The term 'food intolerance' describes an adverse reaction to chemicals in food. The chemicals may be those that are naturally occurring or additives in processed food.

Food intolerance can occur at any age, and reactions usually depend on the amount of a particular food that has been eaten. A toddler or child may show no symptoms after eating the food in small doses or a one-off dose, but may react after eating or drinking a larger amount following a build-up of the chemical(s) over time.

Commonly recognised symptoms of intolerance are not that different from allergy symptoms and include hives, rashes, itching, migraines, irritable bowel, asthma, nasal congestion, abdominal cramps and diarrhoea, lethargy and limb pains.

Diagnosing food intolerance can only be done by an elimination diet followed by a food challenge. This takes a long time and involves very restricted diets, a difficult feat for young children – not to mention their parents. Results can be ambiguous – it is often hard to know whether a reaction is due to the challenge or to chance.

A tricky business

The issue of food allergy and intolerance becomes very confused in relation to babies and toddlers because they can't explain what is troubling them. All toddlers at some time or another suffer from the endless runny nose, the eternal cough, runny poo and mysterious rashes. Toddlers also tend to behave in unpredictable ways, eat like birds and poo like elephants – none of which are symptoms of anything other than being a toddler.

To add to the confusion, research into the relationship between food and common childhood ailments such as asthma, eczema and hay fever is conflicting, and the success of dietary restrictions in alleviating these conditions varies tremendously with individuals. As these ailments tend to come and go spontaneously, it can be very hard to work out how much of a part food plays compared to cigarette smoke, viral infections, dust and air pollution, pollen, dust mites, the weather and animals.

What is Lactose Intolerance?

As with food allergy and intolerance, there has been an over-diagnosis of lactose intolerance in babies and toddlers in the last 20 years, resulting in the unnecessary elimination of dairy products.

Lactose is a sugar which only occurs in the milk of mammals, including humans. Babies of all species produce an enzyme called lactase while they are receiving milk, which helps digest the lactose. Once weaning occurs, lactase is no longer produced in any animals apart from humans. Not all humans continue to produce lactase, however. People from Asia, Mediterranean countries, the Middle East and some Australian Aborigines do not produce lactase after weaning, which means their guts may be unable to digest the lactose found in milk or products made from milk. It is very unusual for people from a Caucasian or Anglo-Saxon background not to produce lactase. People from this ethnic group rarely suffer from genetic lactose intolerance.

It must be emphasised that babies from ethnic groups likely to be lactose intolerant tolerate breastmilk very well and any problems with lactose only start after 3–4 years of age. Proven genetic lactose intolerance present from birth has only ever been identified in a minuscule number of babies. At the current time the lactose intolerance label is given to many babies who cry a lot in the first three to six months after birth.

Apart from genetic lactose intolerance (the failure of the body to produce lactase), temporary lactose intolerance can occur following gut damage. Common reasons for gut damage are infections (viral or bacterial), other medical illnesses or medications. Because the gut is damaged, lactase production is stopped, and wind, nausea and diarrhoea keep recurring if milk products are given. The gut damage is usually temporary (especially following gastroenteritis in babies and toddlers), although serious infections may cause long-term damage. It is usually only necessary to avoid dairy products for a short period of time until the gut heals. The time this takes varies according to the severity of the infection. For most babies and toddlers it is only two to four weeks.

There are degrees of lactose intolerance, so while some toddlers may not be able to drink large amounts of milk in bottles for some time after an attack of diarrhoea, they can tolerate small amounts on cereal, from a cup or in cooking. Yoghurt is usually fine because the lactose is partially broken down by the bacteria which cause the milk to thicken.

A small number of babies are allergic to the *protein* in milk and are unable to tolerate any milk or milk products at all. Like many things related to babies and toddlers, this rare condition is tricky to diagnose and needs expert care from a suitable health professional who can devise a special diet for the baby.

Sensible Precautions When Introducing Food for Non-allergic Babies (the vast majority)

- Avoid egg white until 12 months.
- Avoid peanut products and strawberries until 12 months.
- Avoid cow's milk as the main drink until 12 months, though small amounts in cereal and from a cup are okay after 6 months.
- Avoid honey until 12 months.
- Avoid whole nuts, chunks of hard food such as celery, carrot and so on, until age 4.

CHAPTER 3

Let's Get Real

Feeding babies or children of any age can be one big guilt trip, and the last thing I want to do is contribute to the voyage.

Having been through my own drama of one disastrous breastfeeding experience and one baby whose lips clamped down like a clam shell at the sight of a spoon of food coming, I am only too aware of the pitfalls that await conscientious mothers. I know what it's like to cook and freeze a zillion little ice cubes of nutritious food only to have it completely refused. And to have a child react hysterically to anything green until someone (not me) finally persuaded her to try avocado at the age of 21. It's a long time to wait for your baby to eat her greens . . .

The reason why some babies take to food and make their mothers' lives easy, while others are difficult and highly selective, remains one of life's great mysteries. The notion that mothers can turn reluctant eaters into good eaters by cooking up special little recipes or by having access to some secret knowledge is simply not true. Nothing is worse than carefully cooking nutritious meals and having them continually rejected. If this happens it's best to keep to simple, easily prepared items even if, for a time in your toddler's life, it's the same old thing day after day.

Manufactured baby food has a small part to play in modern life. If you find there are times when it is convenient or your baby prefers it, then use it.

I have never really been of the belief that babies and toddlers need special food. Once the first stage is passed (and even then, many babies can simply partake of items of family food rather than special baby food) the majority of babies and toddlers can eat what the rest of the family eats.

It's probably more helpful to view the nutritional information we all get bombarded with as a guide for *family* eating. Babies and toddlers aren't necessarily going to comply with nutritional guidelines but if they are living in a family where there is a variety of good food offered most of the time, and a reasonable example is set by their parents, they will be fine.

I have included small amounts of sugar, salt, oil, butter and occasionally alcohol, when appropriate, in many recipes. If you feel strongly about not using these items, omit them. I also think most babies can start experiencing the taste of foods such as onions, garlic, basil, tomato sauce and so on from the age of 7–9 months – but again, if for some reason you don't want your baby to start on such items until she is older, do your own thing.

CHAPTER 4

Using the Recipes

Recommended Ages

The suggested ages on the recipes are a guide only.

I have seen babies of 6–7 months eating lumps and chunks with ease. I have seen babies of 12 months who are still being breastfed and just starting to eat finger food. Adapt the food to your baby or toddler. Some recommended ages relate to allergy and food safety guidelines.

Recommended Amounts

It is impossible to be precise about the amount of food babies would or should eat. If your baby or toddler eats like a bird, make sure you offer a birdlike serving. On the other hand, if she loves to eat there is no need to restrict the amount when the food being offered is good-quality food. Quite a few babies eat what seems like a huge amount between 6 and 12 months only to lose interest after that time. The following is an indication only – please adjust for individual appetites and family numbers.

Baby Serve	(2–4 tablespoons)
Toddler Serve	(1–2 cups)
Adult Serve	(1 average adult serve)
Family Serve	(2 average adult serves, 1 toddler serve and 1 baby serve)

Texture – Mash, Mush, Lumps or Chunks?

As with amounts, the texture needed varies between babies. To allow for this I have used the following terms:

PUREE/BLEND

Super smooth. Not a hint of a lump. Processed in an electric blender, Bamix or electric food processor.

MOULI

A coarser texture. Processed in a hand blender or mouli (same name for the same piece of equipment).

MASHED

A much coarser, lumpier texture. Mashed with a fork or potato masher.

FINGER FOOD

Food left whole for your baby or toddler to pick up and eat herself.

CHAPTER 5

Cooking the Food

Kitchen Equipment

POTATO MASHER, GRATER, STRAINER, HAND BEATER AND HAND JUICER

The basics, and likely to be found in any kitchen.

SOME SORT OF ELECTRICAL BLENDER (BAMIX, BLENDER OR FOOD PROCESSOR)

A Bamix is a hand-held implement with various attachments which puree, chop and mix in the container being used (for example, pureeing soup in the pot).

It is much easier to blend small amounts of baby food with a Bamix or a hand blender than in a full-size electric blender or food processor.

Blenders and food processors are very useful in the preparation of family food but are certainly not essential.

MOULI OR HAND BLENDER

A mouli can be a boon. It is inexpensive, can be taken on trips and holidays, is easy to clean after use and excellent for grinding up food that is hard to mash — for example, meat, chicken, pasta and rice.

You need to use plenty of liquid with the food you are putting into the mouli, and it's a good idea to dismantle the mouli and rinse it straight after use.

Buy a good-sized one that has several interchangeable grating discs.

I have to add that there are always going to be some babies who will never eat ground-up food. They either go straight to finger food or get stuck on commercial food (often a combination of both); however, a mouli is also a help in general food preparation and if you don't use it much for one baby, chances are you will with another!

STEAMER

Steaming is a great way to cook vegetables, fruit and sometimes fish and chicken. The food is cooked over boiling water. There are many ways of doing this. Steamer baskets or multi-tiered steamers are available that will steam several items at once. A simple way is to use a colander over a saucepan with a well-fitting lid.

MICROWAVE OVEN

A microwave oven is optional, but they are now found in 70–80 per cent of Australian homes. Microwave cooking is an excellent way to complement conventional cooking, especially when cooking for babies and toddlers, as a microwave oven thaws, cooks and heats food quickly. Microwave cooking reduces the need to use fat and salt, and minimises vitamin and mineral loss so there are also nutritional benefits. Vegetables, fruit and fish cook very well in microwave ovens.

Microwave cookbooks give many recipes and advice on using microwave ovens. When heating or cooking food for your baby or toddler in the microwave, always stir then test the temperature (by taste or on the inside of your wrist) before serving.

Microwaves are not recommended for heating babies' bottles because of the safety aspects – a number of babies in Australia every year end up with burnt mouths because the temperature of the milk is misjudged or because of hot spots in the milk.

COOKING TIPS

Food can be baked, boiled, steamed, cooked in a microwave oven or given raw.

When boiling, add just enough water to cover and simmer gently until the food is tender.

To microwave fruit and vegies, put the food in a microwave or ceramic dish with a teaspoon of water and cover the dish with a lid. Cook on high for about three minutes, stir and cook again for another two minutes. Cooking time obviously varies with the type and amount of fruit and vegies.

The cooking liquid is very useful to use as a moistener when blending, putting food through a mouli or mashing.

Freezing Food

Freezing food saves time and money. However, before you cook and freeze large amounts of food for your baby, wait until you have worked out what she will and won't eat. Here are a few freezing tips.

1. The basics
• Freeze food as soon as possible after purchasing or cooking.
• Never refreeze frozen food that has already been thawed.
• Once thawed, use within 24 hours.
• Use good-quality packaging (freezer bags with air expelled or rigid containers with airtight lids).
• Label and date food at time of freezing.

2. Thawing and reheating
• Whenever possible, defrost or thaw foods in the refrigerator. Alternatively, use a microwave oven.
• Small cuts of meat, fish and frozen vegetables can be cooked in a frozen or semi-frozen state.

3. Foods that freeze well
- Cooked and raw vegetables.
- Cooked fruit.
- Savoury breads such as herb and garlic bread.
- Fish, meat and poultry.
- Lasagne, casseroles and stews.
- Soup and stock.
- Scones, muffins, pastries and cakes.
- White sauce and bechamel sauce.

4. Foods that do not freeze well
- Whole uncooked fruit (including melons) and tomatoes.
- Cucumber.
- Fresh bananas and avocado.
- Baked custards and desserts made with gelatine.
- Fresh cream.
- Raw potato, pumpkin and squash.
- Custard.

5. Freezer storage times

Cooked fruit and vegetables	6 months
Fish	3 months
Uncooked beef, lamb and chicken	6 months
Pork	2 months
Casseroles	1 month
Pasta dishes	1 month
Rice	3 months
Bacon	1 month

6. Freezing small amounts for babies
Common advice for mothers suggests freezing pureed food for babies in ice cubes, popping the ice cubes when frozen into

suitable freezer bags, then using the appropriate number of ice cubes for meals when required. I have never been too keen on this idea. If your baby likes food, it's very easy and rewarding to make fresh food every day or two. If your baby is a fussy eater, you end up with a freezer full of ice cubes no one wants. Cooking up food, freezing it in ice cubes, transferring it to storage bags, getting it out, then defrosting it and heating it, means the food is handled many times before it gets to your baby's mouth.

Cooked food in clean containers or manufactured baby food in jars lasts up to three days in the fridge as long as you always scoop out portions with a clean spoon.

PART TWO

THE FIRST STAGE: 6–7 MONTHS

CHAPTER 6

Starting New Food

The optimum time to start solids changes every decade or so. In the 1920s it was 9 months, in the 1970s it was 6 weeks, in the 1980s it was 3–4 months, in the 1990s it was 4–6 months and now it is 6 months.

Previous recommendations were mostly based on whim, fashion and whatever food was around at the time; now they are mostly based on reliable research and greater scientific knowledge of nutrition, physiology and baby development (we hope). However, cynic that I am, it will be interesting to see what the story is in ten years' time.

Current recommendations from the World Health Organization advise exclusive breastfeeding for the first 6 months whenever possible because:

1. Studies show that by waiting until 6 months the risks of infection and allergic responses in vulnerable babies are reduced.

2. Babies' digestive systems are more mature at 6 months. Their ability to digest starches is limited until then.

3. By waiting until 6 months a range of food can be introduced relatively quickly – as long as the baby is happy to eat it, of

course – rather than stringing the process out over weeks.

4. There are no advantages to starting food other than milk before 6 months (providing an exclusively breastfed baby is getting enough milk for proper growth – see below).

What about Babies on Infant Formula?

As infant formula does not have the immune or the anti-allergic function that breastmilk has, it is difficult to see that point I (on page 35) is relevant. However, points 2, 3 and 4 indicate a slight advantage in waiting until 6 months (as opposed to 4 or 5 months). I don't think they are earth-shattering reasons, but if your baby is happy on formula only, why complicate life before you have to?

It is advisable to offer food at 6 months because:

I. A baby's appetite, nutritional and growth needs are usually no longer satisfied by milk alone.

2. By 6 months babies are starting to chew and bite with their gums. Their hand-to-mouth coordination is more accurate, and between 6 and 9 months they are starting to sit on their own which makes spoon-feeding and finger-food eating easier.

3. The digestive system is more mature.

4. By 6 months many babies are interested in trying a range of food of different consistencies – but not all, of course (see 'Some Normal Variations', pages 42–43).

A Variation on the 6 Months
Breastfeeding 'Rule'

There are a small number of women whose breastmilk diminishes at around 4 to 5 months so that there isn't enough to match their babies' growth needs. This is shown by slow weight gains or no weight gains over four or five weeks (a very thin baby). Often in this situation the breastmilk does not increase despite increasing breastfeeds and getting extra rest. It is important for babies to be adequately nourished, and in my opinion there is nothing to be gained from leaving breastfed babies starving until the magic age of 6 months is reached. As formula in a bottle interferes with breastfeeding, and as these babies often refuse bottles anyway, starting them on rice cereal, fruit and vegies is a good way to give them extra food and still maintain the breastfeeding, which may then continue for the whole of the first year and even beyond.

Food from a spoon is often advised for a range of reasons that have **nothing to do with nutrition**. Here they are:

- **To encourage 'sleeping through', or because the baby suddenly starts waking at night again at around 4–6 months of age**
  Night waking, sadly, is not often related to food. If it were it would provide a nice simple solution for sleep-deprived parents and hassled health workers. Occasionally, in some specific circumstances, it does the trick, but don't be disappointed if you try it and nothing changes. Remember: sleep problems aren't solved by trying to force babies to eat or by searching for the elusive food they will eat.
- **To help prevent reflux vomiting (regurgitation)**
  Starting food from a spoon rarely makes any difference to reflux regurgitation or to crying babies. If your baby is a big regurgitator, you just end up with technicolour vomit instead of white.
- **Curiosity**
  From 3 months on, babies start to become aware of the

world around them and begin to take a great interest in everyday happenings, including what is going into their parents' mouths at mealtimes. Parents become agog with curiosity to see what their baby will do with food of her own and can't wait to try. However, just because babies show interest in the process is not a signal to start giving them food and doesn't necessarily indicate that they want the food themselves. Between 4 and 6 months it's fine to offer them occasional small tastes of food if you want to – for example, a suck on a mandarin or a taste of mashed potato – but if your baby is thriving, wait until 6 months for the main event.

- **The baby starts biting, chewing and sucking on everything in sight, including her fingers and hands**
  From around 3 months, babies' hands are never out of their mouths. This is part of their sensory/motor development and not a sign of needing food. Between 3 and 6 months they all want to bite, chew and suck on anything going – again, this is part of their normal development, unrelated to food or eating, and one way they learn about the world and all it contains.

- **Starting food early makes babies good eaters**
  I have never seen any evidence that this is the case, including times in the past when babies were started on solids at very young ages. Whether or not babies and toddlers are good eaters seems to depend mostly on temperament, a bit on the parents' management of the eating behaviour and a degree of luck.

- **'Big' babies need food earlier**
  Big babies thrive on breastmilk and formula in the first 6 months, the same as any other babies.

- **Pressure from relatives and friends**
  As previously noted, the guidelines for starting solids

change with every generation so it is usual for mothers to be inundated with a range of suggestions from their nearest and dearest accompanied by what can sound like very valid reasons – 'It helps them to sleep at night' and 'It didn't do *you* any harm' are the biggies. However, in light of current knowledge, 6 months for most babies seems to be the optimum time.

What about Premature Babies?

As with full-term babies, the age at which premature babies start eating food and progressing to finger food and a full diet depends to a large extent on the baby.

Babies born 4–6 weeks early will mostly follow the same guidelines.

Babies born 7–12 weeks early can be offered food from around 7 months, but if your premature baby is not interested, or actively dislikes the idea, the best plan is to wait a month and try again. If she doesn't start eating until 9–12 months, so be it – premature babies have the same range of eating behaviours as full-term babies. (See 'Some Normal Variations', pages 42–43.)

Which Food?

Choose from the following. You may start in any order.

- Rice cereal (use any brand or make your own). Use it as a meal on its own or mixed with fruit. Eventually it becomes 'breakfast'. It is not meant to be used as a mixer with all the other food at every mealtime – too much rice can make babies very constipated.
- Lightly cooked apples and pears.
- Mashed or blended avocado.
- Mashed or blended banana.

- Steamed and blended vegetable – try potatoes, carrot and pumpkin to begin with, as they are easy to mash. Once you ascertain that your baby likes vegies, you can branch out and try the full range.
- Yoghurt – full-fat, natural.
- Ricotta cheese.
- Chicken soup.
- Vegie broth.

How to Proceed

Pick one of the items from the above list. Traditionally, rice cereal is the first choice, but feel free to try one of the others if you would rather. If you are using rice cereal, try one or two teaspoons mixed with 15–30 ml of expressed breastmilk, boiled water or prepared formula.

You don't have to sterilise the dish and spoon.

The way babies respond to food varies a lot, and a precise approach leads to tension and unnecessary stress. Don't get too bogged down by the 'rules'. Be flexible, be relaxed and, above all, be guided by your baby.

Try at any time of the day that suits you. It doesn't have to be at the same time every day. Until your baby starts to expect food, it doesn't matter if you miss the food on some days.

If, after a day or two, it's going down with a minimum of fuss, add an extra teaspoon of food every day or two until she is having up to one or two tablespoons at a time.

Try a new food from the list every three days or so. If you want to proceed more slowly, try a new food weekly. When she is happily eating once a day, try a second meal. A week or two later, try a third.

Never try to force the food if your baby doesn't want it. If you have an interested eater, resist the temptation to try everything on the menu in three days. Babies who are interested in eating will be having two to three meals a day and eating all or most of the food on the list in three to six weeks.

The food is given *as well as* the breast or bottle. The breast and bottle feeds do not decrease until your baby is eating a couple of tablespoons three times a day (between 7 and 9 months for many babies). See the meal guides on pages 46–47 and 76–77.

Offer the food at the same time as the milk. If you offer the food in between the milk feeds, you will find you are offering your baby food every two hours – this is time-consuming and unnecessary.

Milk or Food First?

For most babies it doesn't matter. A few situations do exist where it is better to offer the milk first. Here they are:

- When babies of 5 months are given extra food because there is not quite enough breastmilk.
- If you and your baby are happier for her to suck first, then by all means do it that way. Initially your baby will probably want to suck when she's hungry – that's what she's used to. Offering her a spoon first may frustrate and annoy her. Giving one breast or half the bottle, then the food, then finishing off with milk suits a lot of babies.

Once spoon-feeding is well under way, most babies who enjoy food usually like to eat first then finish off their meal with the breast or bottle. Sucking after the food is calming and pleasurable for you both. It is also a nice time for a cuddle.

What about Commercial Food?

Commercially prepared food is nutritionally sound and convenient, but it is more expensive.

It has no advantages for most babies. Unfortunately, apart from the convenience factor (which is understandable) the other reason manufactured baby food seems to be taking over is because the 'rules' about feeding babies make many parents feel they are unable to give their baby 'the best'.

Commercial baby food does not offer the range of tastes that home-prepared or fresh food does, and when you prepare the food yourself you know exactly what your baby is getting.

The stated aim of baby food manufacturers is to have 80 per cent of babies in Australia eating their food. It would be sad indeed if we had to rely on manufacturers to feed our babies. Use the jars occasionally in combination with family food.

Some babies will only eat commercial food for a while. See page 74 for advice about this.

Some Normal Variations

Wide variations exist across the eating spectrum which have little to do with the mother's feeding techniques. Here are the main ones I have observed:

1. Loves food, eats anything
Some babies just open up and down it goes. Heaven!

2. Eats well then suddenly refuses
Don't panic. Stop completely and try again in a few weeks. Continue milk only for the time being.

3. Complete refusal
It doesn't matter. If, after you try a few different things over a week or two and you are getting nowhere, *stop* – try again in another week or two. Continue milk only for the time being.

4. Loves some things, refuses others

Give her what she likes, but keep offering new food every so often. Avoid the temptation to try sugary baby biscuits, flavoured custards and added sugar to vary the diet to encourage eating. Quite a number of babies will not eat vegies. If the vegie refusal looks like it's here to stay for a while, it's best to stop offering them every day because you will get angry and your baby will get stressed. Just offer two meals a day or think of something else for the third.

5. Keeps refusing all food from a spoon indefinitely

About 20 per cent of all babies are finger-food babies who constantly refuse food until *they* can feed themselves with their fingers.

Naturally parents find this frustrating, but it's their baby's decision and the only rational approach is to respect this. If you have a finger-food baby, start to allow her two or three pieces of food to suck herself as soon as she is old enough to sit in a high chair. After ten minutes call it quits until the next mealtime. Sometimes finger food gets eaten, sometimes it gets thrown around the room, but healthy babies who eat like this thrive when left to get on with it without a lot of agonising over the five food groups. Offer the breast or bottle after the food.

See pages 133–5 for finger food suggestions.

6. No food at all for a long time

A number of very healthy breastfed babies have mothers with such an abundant milk supply that they refuse to eat anything and end up exclusively breastfed until they are 9–12 months old. These babies usually thrive, so stay relaxed about it.

If you are worried, talk it over with your early childhood nurse or paediatrician. If anyone's advice puts you in panic mode, seek a second opinion.

How Do You Know if the Food Causes a Reaction or Doesn't Suit Your Baby?

It is not always easy to know when food is the cause of problems in babies and toddlers (see pages 15–23). Things like runny noses, loose poo, red cheeks, nappy rash, vomiting, grizzling and night sleep problems often have nothing to do with diet. If you are concerned, stop the food, wait a month and try again.

The following things are stronger indications of possible problems:

- Mountainous vomiting one or two hours after the food in a baby who does not normally vomit much.
- A sudden bout of loose poo which causes a red, burnt bottom. Remember, recycled food in the poo (see page 45) is normal for all babies and toddlers.
- Hives. (Food is a common cause of hives, but not the only one – drugs and infections can also cause hives.)
- Swelling and redness around the mouth soon after the food is eaten.
- A red mottled rash covering the whole body appearing soon after the food is eaten.

Seek advice if you are worried. A small number of babies need supervised, restricted diets because of allergy and intolerance to certain foods.

Constipation

Constipation is not *how often* your baby goes, but what it's like when she does go. If her poo is hard and dry like a rock or small pebbles it means she is constipated.

Breastfed babies often get constipated initially when they start eating food. Here are a few suggestions:

- If your baby is just as happy without the food, stop for a few weeks. When her poo goes back to normal, start the food again.
- Stop rice cereal for a while — cooked pureed pears or ripe mashed paw-paw helps.
- Banana constipates — stop the banana.
- Increase fluids where possible (extra breastfeeds or water).
- Try diluted prune juice in a bottle (half water, half prune juice). If your baby doesn't drink from a bottle, put undiluted prune juice in with fruit and/or yoghurt.
- A little sugar in her cooked fruit or on cereal helps too.

Recycled Food in the Poo

Once babies are eating a wide variety of food, quite a lot of it appears in the poo in its original state, so don't be surprised to see carrots, crusts or spinach. This is quite normal — there's no need to change the diet.

FIRST STAGE BASIC DIET

- A guide to follow when your baby is eating well. Use this guide to get started.
- The age range for this guide is from 6–7 months.
- Offer two or more tablespoons of food two or three times a day.
- 'Lunch' and 'dinner' may be swapped around – vegies are fine to offer in the evening.
- Remember, some babies refuse food or are very selective for up to 12 months.

EARLY MORNING
ANYTIME FROM 4:30–6 a.m.

Breastfeed or bottle feed

MID-MORNING
ANYTIME FROM 9–11 a.m.
'Breakfast'

Breastfeed or bottle feed
Here are some suggestions:
Fruit and Cereal Mix/Apple Tapioca/Prune and Apricot Puree/Tapioca and Banana

---

EARLY AFTERNOON
ANYTIME FROM 1–3 p.m.
'Lunch'

Breastfeed or bottle feed
Here are some suggestions:
Pureed Vegetables/Baby Pumpkin Soup/Rice and Vegie Puree/Gabe's Gourmet Mush

---

EARLY EVENING

ANYTIME FROM 4:30–7 p.m.

'Dinner'

Breastfeed or bottle feed

Here are some suggestions:

Banana on its own/ Avocado and Orange Combo/Avocado and Yoghurt/Chicken Soup or Stock and Rice Cereal/Ricotta Cheese and Stewed Fruit

LATE EVENING

Breastfeed or bottle feed (if needed)

This guide only offers four breastfeeds a day. If you wish to breastfeed more, continue in the way that suits you and your baby.

CHAPTER 7

First Stage Recipes

All these recipes are suitable for your baby from 6 months onward. They are also suitable for breastfed babies who need food before 6 months (4 months onward).

Rice Cereal

Make rice powder by grinding up 2 cups of rice in a blender, coffee or spice grinder (½ cup at a time). Store in an airtight container in the fridge.

Another option is to buy ground rice (available in the supermarket) and make according to instructions on the packet.

Use brown or white rice

TO MAKE THE RICE CEREAL

1. Mix ¼ cup of rice with 1 cup of made-up formula or breastmilk, or a combination of breastmilk and water, in a heavy saucepan and cook over a low heat, bringing the mixture to the boil while stirring constantly. It's quite okay to use cow's milk once your baby is over 6 months.

2. Simmer until creamy (about 4–5 minutes), continuing to stir. Add a little extra liquid if it is too thick.

This is roughly enough for 2 servings depending on your baby's appetite. Refrigerate what you don't need. Reheat the next day using a little more liquid if it needs thinning.

Fruit

Cooked Fruit
• 1–2 BABY SERVES • SUITABLE FOR FREEZING

Generally, fruit should be lightly cooked for babies when it is their first food; however, ripe banana, avocado and paw-paw can be given raw and, as they become used to food, other well-ripened fruit can be given raw, either grated or mashed or in small pieces. Pieces of fresh soft fruit (avoid whole raw apple) can be given as finger food once babies are over 6 months.

apples
pears
peaches

1. Remove the skin, core, seeds or stone.
2. Cut into small pieces or slices.
3. Put into a saucepan with just enough water to cover the fruit.
4. Cook gently, with the lid on, over a low to medium heat for 5–6 minutes, or until the fruit is tender.
   Or to microwave – put in a microwave-safe dish with 1 tablespoon water. Cover and cook on high for 5–7 minutes. Alternatively, steam fruit in a vegetable steamer.
5. According to what your baby likes, mash or puree the cooked fruit using a little of the cooking liquid if necessary. Remember, babies prefer food to be fairly moist.

Dried Fruit

Remove any stones and soak for 2 hours, or overnight, in cold water. Cook in the same way as described for fresh fruit.

VARIATIONS
- Try combinations of fruit such as pears and apples.
- Simmer apples with a cinnamon stick. Don't forget to remove the cinnamon stick before mashing or blending.

Raw Apple Puree
• 2–4 BABY SERVES • SUITABLE FOR FREEZING

2 ripe apples
30 ml apple juice or orange juice

1. Peel, core and chop apples.
2. Puree with apple juice.

Fruit and Cereal Mix
• 1–2 BABY SERVES

Babies often enjoy fruit with cereal as it is tastier than cereal on its own. Adding cereal to fruit makes a more substantial meal for hungry babies.

1 tablespoon pureed fruit
1 tablespoon rice cereal

1. Mix 1 tablespoon of fruit with 1 tablespoon of rice cereal.
2. Add extra fluid (water, breastmilk, formula or unsweetened fruit juice) to make a suitable consistency for your baby.

Prune Juice

60 g (about 10–12) prunes
375 ml (1½) cups cold water

1. Soak the prunes in water for about 2 hours.
2. Strain soaking liquid into a saucepan. Bring to boil and add prunes.
3. Simmer for 10 minutes or until tender.
4. Strain the juice from the pulp – it should be a good rich brown colour – and store in a clean covered container in the refrigerator.

Prune and Apricot Puree
• 1–2 BABY SERVES • SUITABLE FOR FREEZING

An excellent mix for babies having a few hard poo problems (see pages 44–45).

6 prunes
6 dried apricots

1. Soak prunes and apricots in cold water for about 2 hours. Drain.
2. Put into a saucepan without a lid. Barely cover with cold water, bring to the boil and simmer, stirring occasionally until tender and most of the liquid has evaporated.
3. Drain, remove the stones and blend or mouli.

Apple Tapioca
• 1–2 BABY SERVES • SUITABLE FOR FREEZING

1 tablespoon tapioca
½ cup (120 ml) apple juice
2 tablespoons apple puree

1. Put tapioca and apple juice in a small saucepan.
2. Stir over low heat until the liquid is almost absorbed.
3. Add apple puree.
4. Stir, cool and serve.

VARIATIONS
• Substitute the apple juice with orange juice.
• Substitute the apple puree with pear or peach puree.

Stewed Fruit
• SUITABLE FOR FREEZING

If your baby likes cooked pureed fruit you might like to cook up a variety of fruit combinations and freeze them in serving portions. (See notes on freezing – pages 30–32.)

For each 500 g allow:
½ cup white sugar
⅓ cup water with very juicy, soft fruit (such as berries)
½ cup water with ripe, juicy fruit (such as peaches, apricots, rhubarb)
1 cup water with firm, less juicy fruit (such as apples)
2 cups water with dried fruit – soak dried fruit for about 2 hours first
1 tablespoon lemon juice adds to the flavour
suitable fresh fruit or dried fruit such as apples, pears, peaches,

nectarines, plums or apricots (on their own or in combinations –
for example, apple and pear, apricots and plums, and so on).

1. Prepare the fruit by removing skin and seeds as appropriate and roughly chop.
2. Put into a saucepan with sugar and water; cover and stew
gently until the fruit is tender.

COOKING TIMES
Soft fruit – up to 10 minutes
Hard fruit – up to 20 minutes
Dried fruit – up to 30 minutes
3. Mash, press through a mouli or blend in a food processor
or blender. (This may have to be done in batches.)
4. Freeze in serving portions.

Fruit Gel
• 1–2 BABY SERVES • SUITABLE FOR FREEZING

1½ level teaspoons gelatine
½ cup (120 ml) boiled water
½ cup (120 ml) fruit juice

1. Dissolve gelatine in water.
2. Add fruit juice and mix well.
3. Pour mixture into a bowl. Cover.
4. Let cool. Store in refrigerator to set.

Yoghurt
Yoghurt is an excellent first food for babies, either on its own,
or added to fruit or vegetables.

Yoghurt served with fresh fruit makes a good meal for older
babies.

The healthiest yoghurt for babies is natural full-fat yoghurt; however, the fruit yoghurts are fine to try if your baby is not keen on the natural ones.

There are many commercial brands of yoghurt available to try that are all satisfactory.

Commercial baby yoghurt desserts are a diluted version of the real thing. They contain 26 per cent yoghurt, which is then sterilised so the yoghurt's culture is destroyed, then mixed with fruit juice. They are fine to use as an alternative now and then, or to start with, but are not as nutritious or as versatile as full-fat yoghurt.

Ricotta Cheese

Ricotta cheese can be a good starting point for introducing food to babies (a change from the ubiquitous rice cereal).

It can be used as a basis for a variety of starter recipes. Use with fruit or vegies. Here's a sample recipe.

Gabe's Gourmet Mush
• 1–2 BABY SERVES • SUITABLE FOR FREEZING

1 zucchini
1 tablespoon ricotta cheese
sprinkle of grated Parmesan cheese
natural yoghurt for extra liquid, if needed

1. Cut the zucchini into thick slices and steam until soft.
2. While still hot, blend with ricotta cheese and a sprinkle of Parmesan to taste.
3. Add natural yoghurt if necessary.

VARIATIONS

- Substitute ½ cup cubed pumpkin, carrot or sweet potato for zucchini.
- Leave out the Parmesan cheese and used steamed apples or pears, or fresh paw-paw, rockmelon or peaches.

Avocado

Avocado pears are extremely nutritious (the apple from the Garden of Eden) and are enjoyed by many babies. They are excellent on their own but are very versatile and can be used in many combinations with other food. Some babies find them a little rich, which can result in a bright green vomit. If this happens, wait a few weeks before trying again.

Avocado on its own
• 1–2 BABY SERVES • NOT SUITABLE FOR FREEZING

1. Scoop out ¼ avocado.
2. Mash well with a fork or push through a strainer if your baby wants it really smooth.
3. Serve immediately before it goes brown.

Avocado and Yoghurt
• 1–2 BABY SERVES • NOT SUITABLE FOR FREEZING

¼ avocado
1 tablespoon yoghurt

1. Mash avocado until it is smooth.
2. Mix in yoghurt and serve immediately.

Avocado / Orange Combo

• 1–2 BABY SERVES • NOT SUITABLE FOR FREEZING

¼ avocado
1 tablespoon orange juice
1 teaspoon rice cereal

I. Mash all the ingredients together until smooth.
2. Serve immediately.

Banana

Mashed or pureed banana with a little orange juice is an excellent first food for babies. It does give some babies hard poo, so if this happens you may have to stop the banana for a little while. Banana also makes a strange poo sometimes, so don't panic if there are a few dark red stringy bits in your baby's poo after she eats a banana – it's harmless.

Banana on its own

• 1–2 BABY SERVES • NOT SUITABLE FOR FREEZING

¼ very ripe banana
small amount breastmilk or made-up formula

I. Mash the banana until smooth or push through a strainer for a really smooth texture.
2. Add a little milk and mix well if it is too thick for your baby.

VARIATIONS

• Try mashed banana with cooked pureed apples and orange juice, or with mashed ripe paw-paw or rockmelon. Add orange juice and/or a teaspoon of yoghurt. Mix well or puree in a blender or food processor.

Tapioca and Banana
• **1–2 BABY SERVES** • **NOT SUITABLE FOR FREEZING**

3 tablespoons cooked tapioca (according to instructions on packet)
½ small ripe banana
1 tablespoon breastmilk or made-up formula

I. Blend all of the ingredients together for a smooth consistency, or mash together with a fork for a textured consistency.

Lightly Cooked Vegetables

I suggest potato, pumpkin and carrot to begin with as they are all easy to cook and mash or puree. You can try them separately or combine them. Babies often like potatoes and pumpkin together. Once you have established that your baby is going to be a vegie eater, try the full range of vegies in various combinations. You do not have to give one new vegie weekly to test the result – it would take a year to try them all!

Many vegetables and fruit contain beta carotene. Beta carotene is a yellow pigment that is converted by the body into vitamin A. If your baby starts to eat any substantial amount of foods such as pumpkin, carrots, spinach, tomatoes, peaches, apricots and prunes, you may find her skin has a yellow tinge. The yellow skin is harmless and there is no need to reduce the offending items as they are all good for your baby. Beta carotene does not have this effect on the skin after age 3.

Vegetable dishes are very suitable for microwave ovens.

For any of the following recipes that require cooking of vegetables:

I. Dice vegetables into small pieces.

2. Place in a microwave-safe bowl with a small amount of water – just enough to cover the surface of the bowl.

3. Cover and cook on high for 3–5 minutes.

4. Mash in the bowl and serve.

Pureed Vegetables
• 2–3 BABY SERVES • SUITABLE FOR FREEZING

Vegetables may be cooked, pureed, and served separately or together in combinations. Here are the basic steps.

1 medium potato
1 medium chunk of butternut pumpkin or 1 small carrot
1 zucchini

1. Peel vegetables and cut into similar-sized pieces.

2. Steam, boil or microwave the vegetables until they are tender.

3. Mash, blend or mouli with any cooking liquid, breastmilk or made-up formula to a smooth, creamy-thick texture.

VARIATIONS

- A combination of potato with a red/orange vegetable and a green vegetable in equal quantities is a good balanced mixture. Try potato, pumpkin, zucchini, spinach, broccoli, sweet potato, green beans, cauliflower, cabbage and tomato in various combinations.
- Use yoghurt or a small amount of butter as a mixer.

Baby Pumpkin Soup

• 1–2 BABY SERVES • SUITABLE FOR FREEZING

250 g pumpkin, peeled and chopped
2 tablespoons chopped parsley
¼ teaspoon ground nutmeg
½ cup cooked white rice
2 cups water or homemade stock (see pages 60–62)

1. Place all the ingredients in a saucepan. Cover and bring to the boil. Reduce heat. Simmer, covered for 15–20 minutes, or until tender.
2. Blend until smooth.

VARIATION
• Use 1 cup chopped mixed vegetables in place of the pumpkin for a baby vegetable soup.

Rice and Vegie Puree

• 1–2 BABY SERVES • NOT SUITABLE FOR FREEZING

½ cup cooked rice
½ tomato, peeled, seeded and chopped
1 tablespoon ricotta cheese
1 tablespoon cooked peas
a little breastmilk, made-up formula or water

1. Combine rice, tomato, ricotta cheese and peas.
2. Mash, blend or mouli according to your baby's preference.

Chicken Stock/Soup

Stock is the basis for many recipes and homemade stock brings an excellent flavour to other dishes. However, if you haven't any homemade stock on hand, try one of the following:

- Butchers often have frozen stock in containers for sale. (My butcher's stock is delicious.)
- Use water with a dash of Vegemite.
- Tomato puree or vegetable juices suit some recipes.
- Liquid stock is available in the supermarket in up to 4-cup packs. They are relatively expensive but are more like home-made stock.

If you'd rather, just use water.

Chicken Stock
• SUITABLE FOR FREEZING

1 chicken carcass or bones
chicken giblets (optional)
2 carrots, scrubbed and coarsely chopped
1 onion, quartered
1 leek
3–4 stalks celery, coarsely chopped
3 sprigs parsley
1 bay leaf
2 litres water

1. Place chicken carcass, chicken giblets, vegetables and herbs in a large pan.
2. Add the water; bring to the boil and skim the froth from the top.
3. Cover and simmer for 1–2 hours.
4. Cool, strain and chill overnight.
5. Remove any congealed fat from the surface of the stock the next day.
6. Refrigerate for up to 3 days or freeze immediately.

Vegetable Stock
• SUITABLE FOR FREEZING

1 onion, peeled and quartered
2 carrots, scrubbed and coarsely chopped
3 stalks celery, coarsely chopped
3 sprigs parsley
1 bay leaf
1 bouquet garni (optional, see note)
½ teaspoon tomato paste
a few black peppercorns
2 litres water

1. Place all the ingredients in a large pan with the water.
2. Bring to the boil, cover and simmer for about 1 hour.
3. Allow the mixture to cool.
4. Strain the stock into a bowl and discard the vegetables.
5. Refrigerate for up to 3 days or freeze immediately.

Note: A bouquet garni is a bunch of herbs, such as parsley, bay leaf and celery, tied together so that they can be easily removed.

Beef Stock
• SUITABLE FOR FREEZING

2–3 kg beef bones or a cheap cut of beef (such as 500 g chuck or gravy beef, cubed)
2 stalks celery
1 large carrot, unpeeled, or any vegies to hand such as parsnip, turnip or pumpkin
2 brown onions, unpeeled
1 teaspoon black peppercorns
2 bay leaves
2 litres water

1. Wash and dry the bones if using.
2. Place meat or bones in a large pan and cover with 2 litres cold water.
3. Cut vegetables into chunks and place in the pan.
4. Add the peppercorns and bay leaves.
5. Slowly bring to the boil. Cover and simmer for 4 hours.
6. Skim off any grey scum, and remove vegetables, bones and meat. Strain the stock carefully.
7. Skim the surface again to remove fat and scum. Paper towels are useful for this.
8. Store in the refrigerator or freeze for up to 2 months.

Betsy Berger's Chicken Soup

Chicken soup is a regular item in the homes of many of the families I see. Traditionally in families of European descent this wonderful nourishing dish is offered as baby's first food, often made by doting grandmothers.

Betsy is the mother of four children who have all visited me throughout their baby and toddler years. Chicken soup is a regular item in their home and all Betsy's babies enjoyed rice cereal mixed with the broth from this soup as their first food.

8 chicken wings or drumsticks
8 stalks celery, sliced
8 large carrots, peeled and sliced
1 parsnip, peeled
1 turnip, peeled
2 large onions, peeled
4 litres homemade chicken stock (see page 60)
1 packet thin egg noodles

1. Place all the ingredients except the noodles in a large pan.
2. Bring to the boil then cover and simmer for 1½–2 hours.
3. Discard the chicken pieces, parsnip, turnip and onion.
4. Skim the fat off the surface.
5. Boil noodles in the soup for 10 minutes.

TO SERVE

For babies' first food: add the stock to rice cereal. Mix well.
For older babies: add the stock to pureed vegetables.
For toddlers: 1 ladleful of soup with noodles.

PART THREE

THE SECOND STAGE: 7–12 MONTHS AND BEYOND

CHAPTER 8

Expanding the Menu

I am aware that parents are very keen to have food arranged neatly in age groups. However, because of the wide range of ways that babies take to food and all the possible options there are to follow, I find in my work it is more helpful to give broader guidelines. Apart from the few foods recommended to delay until 12 months of age, most babies can try most foods by 9 months of age.

A lot of the recipes in this section and the toddler section are family foods that babies and toddlers can share. Some of the recipes given for first stage food may still be favourites when your baby is 12 months old. Some babies will be getting into many of the toddler recipes at 9 months. Finger foods are easier to give when babies can sit on their own — the range for sitting is any time from 6 to 9 months. And, of course, there are the reluctant eaters who are still mostly breastfed and throwing food around the room at 12 months.

It is simply not possible to slot food neatly into age categories once babies are past the first stage. Complicated charts and detailed advice about various foods to be eaten at various ages throughout the first year are not necessary.

I have included a diet plan for the next stage on pages 76–77.

Here is some information to help you with the diet plan:

- Babies who like eating will be following this plan by 9 months. Don't rush things unnecessarily; on the other hand, there's no need to delay introducing a wide variety of food if your baby is enjoying food.
- If allergy is a consideration for you, follow recommendations from your adviser. If you are thinking of restricting your baby's diet in any major way, please seek advice from a knowledgeable health professional so that your baby's diet is nutritionally sound.
- Offer the food before milk from now on if you have been doing the reverse.
- As well as changing from four-hourly feeds to three meals a day, this plan suggests cutting down the breast or bottle feeds to three or four every 24 hours. This will suit lots of mothers and babies, but obviously not all.
  Breastfeeding: If you wish to breastfeed more often, continue in the way that suits you and your baby. Or if you do decide to only breastfeed three times a day, the feeds do not necessarily have to be given according to the plan – again, do what suits you both the best.
  Bottle feeding: Three bottles of milk a day is all your baby needs once she is eating well. Try water at other times when your baby is thirsty (see page 73).
- When your baby has breakfast later, after an early feed, there's no need to repeat the bottle or the breast – a little water from a bottle or a cup with her breakfast is all that is needed.
- If your baby is a 7–8 a.m. waker, give her breakfast as soon as she wakes up, followed by a breastfeed, her bottle or milk from a cup.
- Some breastfed babies whose mothers have an abundant milk supply don't want breakfast after their morning

breastfeed. The breastmilk supplies all they need, so don't worry if your baby does this – she will probably start eating breakfast sometime around 12 months.

Foods to Avoid (non-allergic babies)

- Honey is a form of sugar and, as such, is a problem if given too often. It has been known to cause botulism (poisoning by toxins produced by harmful bacteria) in babies under 12 months, so if you occasionally use honey on bread wait until your baby is over a year old.
- Other foods to avoid include whole apple, whole carrot, raw celery, corn chips or popcorn, because of the risk of choking. It is now recommended that these foods not be given until children are over 4 years.
- Avoid seeds, pips and nuts – all choking hazards. Give plain bread.
- Strawberries can cause an extreme reaction in some babies; wait until she is a year old.
- Peanut products are also responsible for severe reactions in some babies, so wait until 12 months before starting peanut butter.
- Wait until 12 months to give egg white.
- Avoid chilli and 'hot' food.

See page 19 for guidelines for allergic babies.

Food Safety

Food safety precautions are very important as soon as your baby starts eating family food. Once your baby starts eating food herself, make sure she is always supervised and not allowed to crawl or walk with food.

Gagging and Choking

Most parents worry about the way their baby gags at times, and the possibility of her choking, and often confuse gagging with choking. It's a normal worry, but unfortunately it can lead to a baby's diet being too restricted and the delaying of finger foods at the ideal time to start them (between 6 and 9 months).

What's the Difference?

Gagging

Babies are born with a strong gag reflex which is part of their body's natural defence against food entering the respiratory tract instead of the oesophagus. The gag reflex persists throughout life – for example, if you are forced to eat something you don't like you will automatically gag. Babies have to learn to inhibit their involuntary gag reflex when they start eating finger food or food of a much lumpier consistency than they are used to. They also have to learn how much food to put in at a time when they feed themselves – biting off more than they can chew is common. To confuse the issue, the other common thing babies learn to do is to gag voluntarily when they don't wish to eat something. The gagging-on-purpose habit can last well into the toddler years, making parents believe their toddler is physically unable to eat anything other than a liquid diet – forgetting about the times a chocolate biscuit or a packet of chips goes down without a problem.

When a baby gags, the food sits at the back of her throat and either ends up going down where it's supposed to go or comes up again. As long as you are around to make sure she's all right and the food doesn't get stuck, gagging is harmless and part of the way she learns to feed herself and eat lumpier food.

Many babies need the main part of their meal ground up

until they are 12 months old as the gag reflex remains strong and, to some extent, involuntary until then. Lumpy food from a spoon can therefore tend to make mealtimes stressful because the lumps cause a lot of gagging. As mothers are constantly told to offer lumpy food from a spoon from 6 months on, with dire warnings of babies never learning to chew if they don't, I find this a cause of great stress for many families. Oddly enough, when babies feed themselves finger food they control their gag reflex much more efficiently, so a good compromise is to give your baby the main part of her meal ground up, then offer her some finger food she can eat herself. Obviously, if your baby manages chunky food from a spoon without gagging a lot, go for it!

Choking

Choking occurs when the airway is obstructed, preventing air from reaching the lungs. When it is a small, soft item (a crumb or a soft lump) the baby will usually cough, which removes the object from the airway. Serious obstruction happens when the item is a small, hard object like an orange pip, a lolly or a piece of apple which gets 'stuck' in the airway and partially or completely blocks it.

First Aid for Choking

Check first to see if the baby is still able to breathe, cough or cry. If she is breathing, coughing or crying, she may be able to dislodge the food by coughing. Do not try to dislodge the food by hitting the baby on the back, because this may move the food into a more dangerous position and make her stop breathing.

Stay with the baby and see if her breathing improves. If she is not breathing easily within a few minutes, phone 000 for an ambulance.

If the baby is not breathing:

1. Try to dislodge the piece of food by placing the baby face down over your lap so her head is lower than her chest.

2. Give the baby four sharp blows on the back just between the shoulder blades. This should provide enough force to dislodge the food.

3. Check again for signs of breathing.

4. If the baby is still not breathing, urgently call 000 and ask for an ambulance. The ambulance service operator will be able to tell you what to do next.

These guidelines are from Kids Health at the Children's Hospital, Westmead and Sydney Children's Hospital, Randwick, with grateful acknowledgement to the Women's and Children's Hospital in Adelaide.

Note: It is very difficult to learn basic resuscitation techniques from a book. Courses are available in your state from the Royal Life Saving Society, the Red Cross and St John Ambulance, and learning and/or updating your skills is always a very worthwhile thing to do.

If you have an emergency and you don't know what to do, take the baby to the phone and ring the Ambulance Service on 000 (anywhere). The trained operator will give emergency instructions over the phone.

It must be emphasised that choking is not a hazard normally associated with introducing a wide range of food to babies over the age of 6 months as long as you take a few sensible precautions. Try not to let fear of choking put you off allowing your baby to try different foods and different ways of eating.

Teeth and Food

Teeth emerge any time between 3½ months and 16 months. The arrival of teeth has nothing to do with when and what your baby eats. Many 12-month-old babies with no teeth eat a wide variety of chunky food, as they learn to use their gums very efficiently.

Juice

Juice is not necessary. An overabundance of juice sipped throughout the day from bottles through a straw and from spout cups in the last 20 years has led to an increase in toddler diarrhoea and tooth decay and erosion. Juice, however, *is* useful for babies who are constipated (see page 45).

One drink of juice a day is reasonable in a cup to be drunk in one sitting. If you offer it straight after a meal, the vitamin C helps iron absorption. Juice is problematic when it is offered over several hours or, worse, overnight, in bottles or cups with teats, spouts or straws. The juice pools around the teeth, bathing them with sugar that forms plaque, a sticky film that bacteria adhere to — a primary cause of tooth decay.

Water

Water is the ideal drink for babies and toddlers. If they are truly thirsty they will drink it, especially if juice is not immediately offered as an alternative. Town water is best as it often contains fluoride and is relatively inexpensive. Bottled water, one of the crazier innovations of the last 20 years, has no fluoride, no advantages to town water and costs a lot more. Mineral water has high levels of salt and other minerals and is not recommended for babies and toddlers.

On the subject of fluoride

Fluoride protects against tooth decay bacteria, strengthens tooth enamel and is a cost-effective way of minimising the risk of decay for all children. However, there are still areas of Australia where the water supply is not fluoridated. If you live in an unfluoridated area or use a water purifier (some water purifiers eliminate all fluoride, others filter out variable amounts), it is beneficial to give a fluoride supplement.

For children between ages 2 and 4, use a children's low-dose fluoridated toothpaste. Once your child is over 4, check with your dentist about using fluoride tablets or drops. It is important to know the status of your water supply before giving fluoride supplements – too much fluoride will discolour the teeth permanently.

Safe use of fluoride toothpaste
* Do not use fluoride toothpaste until your toddler is 2.
* Children between ages 2 and 6 should use low-fluoride toothpaste. Not all toothpastes made for children contain fluoride, and low-fluoride toothpastes are only available in one or two brands – check with your pharmacist.
* Apply a thin, pea-sized amount of toothpaste to the brush.
* Limit your child's use of fluoride toothpaste to twice daily.
* Keep toothpaste out of the reach of children.

Babies Who Will Only Eat Commercial Food

Remember, you can't force babies to eat things they don't want to eat. Commercial food is nutritious. Stop cooking your own food if your baby is not eating it and the situation is becoming tense. Give her what she likes, but as soon as she can sit for a while in a high chair follow the jar of food with some finger food for her to eat herself. Offer some fresh, easy food (fruit, bread, cheese) regularly.

Premature Babies

Premature babies can follow the same dietary guidelines, although babies born earlier than 34 weeks will take longer to get to the stage of sitting and eating finger food. Babies born very early may not be ready for the second stage until about 12 months, but all premature babies should be offered a variety of food by 12 months.

SECOND STAGE BASIC DIET

- A guide to follow when your baby is aged from 7–12 months.
- Lunch and evening meal ideas are interchangeable.

5– 6 a.m. (or 4:30 if you're unlucky) Breastfeed or bottle feed 180–210 ml

BREAKFAST 7– 9 a.m.

Note: Some babies are not really interested in breakfast until they are older (especially if they have a big early-morning breastfeed).

Vita Brits/Weet Bix/Porridge/Baby Cereal/Fruity Cereal/Baby Muesli/Peach Semolina/Stewed Fruit and Yoghurt
It's okay to use full-fat milk on cereal after 6 months.
Egg Yolk (at 9 months)
Give soft-boiled yolk off a spoon or dipped in bread
Bread or toast fingers (on its own or with a little cream cheese, Vegemite or avocado toast or cheese on toast)

Suggestions
If no early-morning feed, give breastfeed or bottle feed after breakfast. Otherwise, give a drink of water (cup or bottle) or a little milk in a cup, or another breastfeed.

MORNING TEA 10–11 a.m.
(time for a little something)
Morning and afternoon tea is optional – if your baby doesn't want it or is asleep, forget it. Morning tea is a helpful way of filling in a gap when you're changing from Stage 1 to Stage 2. It is also a good time to practise with a cup and finger food.

Water or a breastfeed
Crusket, rusks, bread, muffins
Fresh fruit, cheese stick, rice cake

LUNCH 12–1:30 p.m.
Basic Baby Beef Stew (This forms
the basis of a main meal and can
be made without meat or substitute
tuna or chicken for the meat.)

Some other ideas:
Orange and Carrot Soup
Savoury Potatoes
Cheesy Vegies
Liver Casserole
Creamed Brains
Basic Chicken Casserole
and/or Banana with Creamy Rice
Baked Pear Custard

Breastfeed or bottle feed or cup of milk.
It's okay to give full-fat milk in a cup after 6 months.

AFTERNOON TEA (same as morning tea) 3–4 p.m.
Some babies aged between 6–9 months need a breastfeed or a small bottle
(120ml) at around 4 p.m. – an often trying part of the day – while they are getting
used to their new regime. This can usually be stopped by 9 months.

DINNER 5–7 p.m.
Cheesy Baked Beans and Pumpkin and/or Lentil Soup with Pasta
Fish Pie   Vegetable Combo
Scottish Stew   Macaroni Cheese
Finger Food   Blended family food
Jann's Pumpkin Soup   Simple Bolognaise

Apple and Pear Crumble/Rhubarb and Banana Compote/Yoghurt and stewed or
fresh fruit/Baked Apple Custard

Suggestions
Give water after the meal (in a bottle or cup) or small cup of milk. Give a
breastfeed or bottle feed before bed.

CHAPTER 9

Cereal, Breads and Muffins

In Chapters 9–17, recipes particularly suited to babies aged between 6–9 months are noted; however, this does not mean that babies of this age cannot try any of the other recipes. Nor does it mean babies over 9 months cannot use the recipes marked 6–9 months.

Cereals

Once babies are over 6 months a variety of cereals can be tried.

Weet-Bix or Vita Brits are easy. Start with ½ or 1 (depending on your baby). Add warm whole cow's milk or, if you prefer, stick with formula.

OTHER IDEAS

- Add a little wheatgerm to the Weet-Bix or Vita Brits.
- Add fresh or cooked, mashed or pureed fruit.
- Add prune juice and a sprinkle of brown sugar if your baby is having hard poo problems.

Basic Porridge
BREAKFAST
• 1 BABY SERVE • SUITABLE FOR BABIES 6–9 MONTHS

1 tablespoon rolled oats
¼ cup water or half milk, half water

1. Combine the rolled oats and liquid in a saucepan.
2. Bring to the boil.
3. Turn heat down and simmer gently for 5 minutes, stirring occasionally. Add extra water if necessary.

Microwave Porridge
BREAKFAST
• 1 BABY SERVE • SUITABLE FOR BABIES 6–9 MONTHS

¼ cup oats
¼ cup milk/¼ cup water (or ½ cup milk)

1. Mix the oats and liquid in a microwave-safe cereal bowl.
2. Microwave on high for 2 minutes, stopping to stir after 1 minute.

Porridge may be served with milk or yoghurt, a sprinkle of wheatgerm, or fresh or cooked, mashed or pureed fruit. Prune juice and a sprinkle of brown sugar helps if your baby is having a few hard poo problems.

Try substituting apple juice for water or milk. Add a pinch of ground cinnamon.

Grinding the dry oats in a blender means they cook faster and make a smoother consistency, which many babies prefer. After grinding, store them in an airtight container.

Baby Muesli
BREAKFAST

• 1 BABY SERVE • SUITABLE FOR BABIES 6–9 MONTHS

⅓ cup rolled oats
½ cup wheatgerm
¾ cup apple juice
1 tablespoon orange juice
2 tablespoons fruit puree (apples, pears or combination)
sprinkle of sugar or ground cinnamon

1. Combine the rolled oats, wheatgerm and apple juice. Cover and refrigerate overnight.
2. Next morning, stir in the orange juice, pureed fruit and sugar or cinnamon.
3. Blend to a smooth texture in a food processor or blender, and serve.

Fruity Cereal
BREAKFAST

• 1 BABY SERVE • SUITABLE FOR BABIES 6–9 MONTHS

1 tablespoon suitable packet cereal (avoid highly sugared or nutty cereals)
1 tablespoon pureed fruit
1 tablespoon natural yoghurt

1. Put all the ingredients into a blender or food processor and blend or mix until smooth.

Breads

Rusks

• SUITABLE FOR BABIES 6–9 MONTHS • SNACK/FINGER FOOD

5 thick slices wholemeal bread

1. Preheat the oven to 150°C.
2. Remove crusts from the bread.
3. Cut the bread into fingers.
4. Put bread on a baking tray and bake for about 1 hour.
5. Cool and store in an airtight container.
Makes about 20 rusks.

VARIATION

• Spread a small amount of Vegemite onto the bread before baking.

Edna's Apricot Loaf

1 cup All Bran
1 cup brown sugar
1 cup dried apricots, chopped
1 cup milk
1 tablespoon honey
1 cup self-raising flour, sifted

1. Preheat the oven to 180°C. Line a loaf tin with non-stick baking paper.
2. Mix the All Bran, brown sugar and apricots together.
3. Warm the milk in a large saucepan and combine with honey, All Bran, brown sugar and apricots.
4. Gradually add the flour and mix well, using a wooden spoon.
5. Pour into the prepared tin and bake for 50 minutes.

Muffins

As babies become toddlers, muffins make great snacks either when you are on the move or for friends who drop in with little ones. They can be frozen and defrosted quickly in the oven and are a good alternative to biscuits.

Here are some general tips on muffin making:

- For baby-size muffins, use mini-muffin trays which make smaller muffins.
- Lightly grease the muffin tray and preheat the oven to recommended temperature before you start mixing.
- Stir muffin mixture with a wooden spoon. The trick is not to overstir – try to make them in less than 15 minutes.
- Apple or pear juice concentrate, used in these muffin recipes, is available in health food shops or supermarkets.

Gabe's Apple Muffins
• MAKES ABOUT 24 MINI MUFFINS

2 cups self-raising flour
1 teaspoon ground cinnamon
½ cup brown sugar
1 cup milk
125 g unsalted butter, melted
1 egg, beaten
2 apples, cored, peeled and roughly grated

1. Preheat the oven to 200°C. Lightly grease two 12-hole mini-muffin trays.
2. Sift the flour and cinnamon together into a mixing bowl.
3. Stir in the sugar.
4. Add the milk, butter, egg and apple.
5. Mix together with a wooden spoon until combined.

82

6. Spoon evenly into the muffin trays.

7. Bake for 15–20 minutes or until golden brown.

8. Remove the muffins immediately from the trays and allow to cool on a wire cooling rack.

Berry Soy Muffins
• MAKES 12 REGULAR OR 24 MINI MUFFINS

2½ cups self-raising flour

375 g berries (blackberries, cranberries, raspberries or blueberries)

½ cup vegetable oil

½ cup pear juice concentrate

¾ cup soy liquid

3 eggs, lightly beaten

1. Preheat the oven to 200°C. Lightly grease the muffin tray.

2. Sift the flour into a mixing bowl and add the berries.

3. In another bowl, combine the vegetable oil, pear juice concentrate, soy liquid and eggs and beat well.

4. Stir the liquid mixture into the flour and fruit mixture.

5. Spoon into the muffin tray and bake for 20–25 minutes or until golden brown.

6. Remove the muffins immediately from the tray and allow to cool on a wire cooling rack.

Gluten Free Apricot Muffins
• MAKES 12 REGULAR OR 24 MINI MUFFINS

Rice flour and soy flour are made from ground rice and ground soybeans and are available in health food shops and many supermarkets.

1 cup soy flour
1 cup rice flour
3 teaspoons baking powder
1 teaspoon ground cinnamon
425 g can apricots
½ cup vegetable oil
¼ cup buttermilk
2 eggs

1. Preheat the oven to 160°C and lightly grease the muffin tray.
2. Put the flours, baking powder and cinnamon into a mixing bowl.
3. Drain the apricots, reserving 1 cup of juice. Roughly chop the apricots and add to the dry ingredients.
4. In another bowl, combine the apricot juice, oil, buttermilk and eggs and beat together.
5. Fold liquid into the flour and fruit and mix together with a wooden spoon.
6. Spoon into the muffin tray and bake for 30 minutes or until golden brown.
7. Remove the muffins immediately from the tray and allow to cool on a wire cooling rack.

Milk and Wheat Free Muffins
• MAKES 12 REGULAR OR 24 MINI MUFFINS

1⅓ cups rye flour
⅔ cup rice flour
4 teaspoons baking powder
¼ teaspoon salt
3 teaspoons sugar
1 cup soy liquid
⅓ cup vegetable oil
1 egg, beaten

1. Preheat the oven to 200°C and lightly grease the muffin tray.
2. Put dry ingredients together in a mixing bowl.
3. Combine remaining liquid ingredients in a small bowl and add to dry ingredients.
4. Stir liquid into dry ingredients, using a fork.
5. Spoon into muffin tray.
6. Bake for 20–25 minutes or until golden.
7. Remove the muffins immediately from the tray and cool on a wire cooling rack.

Milk, Wheat and Egg Free Muffins
• MAKES 12 OR 24 MINI MUFFINS

1⅓ cups rye flour
⅓ cup rice flour
4 teaspoons baking powder
¼ teaspoon salt
3 teaspoons sugar
1¼ cups soy liquid
⅓ cup vegetable oil

1. Preheat the oven to 200°C and lightly grease the muffin tray.
2. Put dry ingredients together in a mixing bowl.
3. Combine remaining liquid ingredients in a small bowl and add to the dry ingredients.
4. Stir liquid into dry ingredients until well combined. Do not beat.
5. Spoon into muffin tray.
6. Bake for 20–25 minutes or until golden.
7. Remove the muffins immediately from the tray and cool on a wire cooling rack.

CHAPTER 10

Fruit

Fruit is a good source of a wide range of vitamins, minerals and natural fibre, and, with vegetables, is the only source of vitamin C. It is ideal as a snack in between meals as it does not diminish the appetite the way biscuits do.

Fruit makes excellent finger food once your baby is at the finger food stage (6–12 months). Try slices of well-ripened pear, rockmelon, watermelon, honeydew melon, mango, peaches, apricots. Grated apple is fine and it's okay to try small pieces of mandarin or orange (make sure all the pips are removed). Fruit as finger food can be given after a meal or in between meals as a snack.

Here are some recipes that use fruit. These recipes can be used as one of the main meals rather than as a dessert while your baby is learning to enjoy food (6–9 months). Older babies who like to eat can have fruit as a dessert after their savoury first course.

To peel fruit such as peaches, nectarines or apricots, put into boiling water for 1 minute, drain and cover with cold water, then drain and remove the skin.

Apple and Pear Crumble
LUNCH OR DINNER
• 2–3 BABY SERVES • SUITABLE FOR BABIES 6–9 MONTHS
• SUITABLE FOR FREEZING

1 pear and 1 apple, peeled, cored and chopped
1 tablespoon caster sugar
¼ teaspoon ground cinnamon
1 cup plain flour
60 g unsalted butter, chopped
¼ cup brown sugar

1. Preheat the oven to 200°C.
2. Place the fruit in a greased ovenproof dish and sprinkle with caster sugar and cinnamon.
3. Sift the flour into a mixing bowl. Rub in the butter until the mixture is crumbly. Stir in the brown sugar.
4. Sprinkle the crumble topping over the fruit.
5. Bake for 40 minutes.
6. Serve with natural yoghurt or custard. If necessary, mash or blend before serving to baby.

VARIATIONS
- Substitute 2–4 stalks of rhubarb for pears and apple.
- Replace ½ cup plain flour with ½ cup rolled oats and 1 tablespoon wheatgerm.

Banana with Creamy Rice
LUNCH OR DINNER
• 1–2 BABY SERVES • SUITABLE FOR BABIES 6–9 MONTHS

½ small banana
a pinch ground cinnamon
1 tablespoon leftover rice pudding (see recipe page 131)
1 tablespoon natural yoghurt

1. Mash the banana.
2. Mix with the cinnamon, rice pudding and yoghurt.
3. Blend or mouli if necessary.

VARIATION
• Substitute pureed pears, apples or apricots for banana.

Rhubarb and Banana Compote
LUNCH OR DINNER
• 2–3 BABY SERVES • SUITABLE FOR BABIES 6–9 MONTHS

2 cups chopped rhubarb
2 tablespoons sugar
½ cup water
½ banana, mashed

1. Simmer the rhubarb with sugar and water for 5–7 minutes.
2. Cool.
3. Stir in the mashed banana and serve with natural yoghurt
or custard.

VARIATIONS
• Substitute ½ cup orange juice for ½ cup water.
• Substitute apple puree or grated apple for banana.

Dried Fruit Compote
BREAKFAST, LUNCH OR DINNER
• 2 ADULT PORTIONS/4 TODDLER PORTIONS • SUITABLE FOR FREEZING

⅓ cup stoned prunes
½ cup dried apricots
⅓ cup dried peaches
1 cup dried apples
½ cup water
2 tablespoons sugar
¼ teaspoon ground cinnamon
½ cup apple juice

1. In a bowl, soak the dried fruit in the water for about 2 hours.
2. Transfer the fruit and liquid to a heavy-based saucepan. Add the sugar, cinnamon and apple juice. Bring to the boil, cover and simmer on a low heat for 20–30 minutes.
3. Leave the mixture to cool.
4. Blend or mouli if necessary.
5. Serve with natural yoghurt.

Mango and Ricotta Mix
BREAKFAST, LUNCH OR DINNER
• 1–2 BABY SERVES • SUITABLE FOR BABIES 6–9 MONTHS

1 ripe mango, peeled and stoned
2 tablespoons ricotta cheese

1. Blend the mango and ricotta cheese together until smooth.

VARIATION
• Substitute paw-paw, banana or pineapple for mango.

Peach Semolina
LUNCH OR DINNER
• 1–2 BABY SERVES • SUITABLE FOR BABIES 6–9 MONTHS

1 cup milk
1 tablespoon semolina
½ teaspoon sugar
1 ripe peach

I. Bring the milk to the boil in a saucepan. Add the semolina and sugar and heat, stirring constantly with a wooden spoon, until the mixture coats the back of the spoon.
2. Serve with mashed, sliced or chopped fresh peach.

VARIATION
• Substitute peach with grated apple or pear.

Baked Pear Custard
LUNCH OR DINNER
• 2 BABY SERVES • SUITABLE FOR BABIES 6–9 MONTHS

Cooked egg white in custard should be fine for most babies of this age. If you are concerned, separate the yolk from the white of the egg.

½ cup pear puree
½ cup milk
1 large egg

I. Preheat the oven to 180°C and grease a small ovenproof dish.
2. Spoon the pear puree into the bottom of the dish.
3. Beat together the milk and egg and pour over the puree.

4. Stand in a small roasting tin with hot water halfway up the dish and bake for 20–30 minutes or until set.

Grandma Dot's Baked Apple Custard
LUNCH OR DINNER
• **1–2 BABY SERVES** • **SUITABLE FOR BABIES 6–9 MONTHS**

This was my first food, which I ate with relish. Sugar was not politically incorrect when I was a baby.

1 cup apple puree
1 cup milk
1 tablespoon sugar
½ teaspoon vanilla flavouring essence
1 egg

1. Preheat the oven to 180°C.
2. Mix the apple puree with the milk, sugar and vanilla flavouring essence.
3. Beat the egg well and stir into the mixture.
4. Pour into a greased ovenproof dish.
5. Bake for 20 minutes or until set.
6. May be served hot or cold.

VARIATION
• Substitute mashed banana for apple puree and add another egg yolk to the egg for more nourishment.

CHAPTER 11

Vegetables and Sauces

Try all the range, either individually or in combinations. Some babies will be able to manage vegies simply mashed with a fork, but most will still prefer them put through a mouli or a blender.

Be adventurous. Try Jerusalem artichoke, celeriac, beetroot, bok choy and choy sum as well as capsicum (red, green and yellow), choko, eggplant, fennel, leeks, parsnip, squash, tomato and turnip.

Like fruit, vegetables make excellent finger food once your baby is at the finger-food stage (6–12 months). Steam them until they are soft but still firm.

Simple ways to vary vegetable meals include mixing grated cheese into hot cooked vegies, adding ricotta, cottage cheese, or natural yoghurt, mixing in some grated hard-boiled egg yolk, or adding some couscous.

Small amounts of finely chopped fresh herbs such as chives, coriander, parsley or dill can be added, as can spices such as ginger, nutmeg or paprika.

To peel tomatoes, put into boiling water for 1 minute before removing the skin.

Vegetables may be moistened with tomato paste or sauce, white sauce, cheese sauce, tahini (sesame seed paste) and hoummos (chick pea dip) or salt-reduced soy sauce.

You will find recipes and information about sauces in this section.

There are also many great recipes using vegetables in Chapter 13 (Soups).

Margaret's Spinach and Rice Pie
LUNCH OR DINNER
• FAMILY SERVE • SUITABLE FOR FREEZING

Two Margarets have contributed to this book. This Margaret is a wonderful midwife and extraordinary bushwalker. She is the fittest person I know and eats very healthy food. This will make your baby spring out of her highchair!

250 g packet frozen spinach, thawed and thoroughly drained
1 cup cooked white rice
3 eggs, beaten
¼ teaspoon ground nutmeg
pepper
1 cup diced fetta cheese
1 tablespoon butter, melted

1. Preheat the oven to 200°C.
2. Combine all the ingredients in a mixing bowl and stir to mix evenly.
3. Spoon into a greased 23 cm round pie plate.
4. Bake for 25 minutes or until set and golden on top.

Savoury Potatoes
LUNCH OR DINNER

• 2 BABY SERVES OR 1 TODDLER SERVE • SUITABLE FOR BABIES 6–9 MONTHS

1 potato, cooked, peeled and diced
½ cup basic tomato sauce (see pages 98–99)
1 teaspoon chopped fresh basil
2 tablespoons Parmesan cheese, to sprinkle

1. Combine the potato, tomato sauce and basil and heat in a microwave oven or a small saucepan over a medium heat.
2. Sprinkle with Parmesan cheese.
3. Mash, blend or mouli according to your baby's preference.

Spinach and Potato Puree
LUNCH OR DINNER

• SUITABLE FOR BABIES 6–9 MONTHS • SUITABLE FOR FREEZING

1 onion, peeled and thinly sliced
30 g butter
1 potato, peeled and chopped
½ cup homemade chicken stock (see page 60)
1 cup cooked spinach or silverbeet

1. Sauté the onion in butter in a heavy-based pan for a few minutes, or until soft.
2. Add the potato and stock, cover and simmer for about 20 minutes.
3. Stir in the spinach and heat through.
4. Mash, blend or mouli according to your baby's preference.

Pureed Triticale and Vegies
LUNCH OR DINNER
• 2 BABY SERVES OR 1 TODDLER SERVE • SUITABLE FOR BABIES 6–9 MONTHS
• SUITABLE FOR FREEZING

½ cup broccoli or cauliflower florets
1 carrot, scraped and sliced
2 mushrooms, brushed, cleaned and diced
1 tablespoon triticale

1. Barely cover all the vegetables with water in a saucepan and add the triticale (see note below).
2. Bring the water to the boil then cover and simmer for 15–20 minutes or until the vegetables are tender.
3. Mash, blend or mouli according to your baby's preference.

Note: Triticale is available from supermarkets and health food shops. It is a new cereal with a flaky consistency and a cross between wheat and rye. Oats can be substituted for triticale.

Cheesy Vegies
LUNCH OR DINNER
• 2 BABY SERVES OR 1 TODDLER SERVE • SUITABLE FOR BABIES 6–9 MONTHS

2 zucchini or squash, trimmed and sliced
1 cup cauliflower florets
1 tablespoon grated tasty cheese
1 egg yolk
1 teaspoon butter

1. Steam the vegetables until they are tender, about 10 minutes, or microwave them in a small amount of water. Reserve the cooking liquid.
2. Add the cheese, egg yolk and butter to the hot

vegetables and mix well. (The egg yolk cooks in the heat of the vegies.)

3. Puree immediately using some of the hot cooking liquid if necessary for extra liquid.

Basic White Sauce
• **MAKES 1 CUP SAUCE** • **SUITABLE FOR FREEZING**

2 tablespoons butter
2 tablespoons plain flour
300 ml full-cream milk, warmed

1. Melt the butter in a small saucepan over low heat.
2. Stir in the flour using a wooden spoon and continue stirring over a low heat for about a minute.
3. Gradually add the milk, stirring constantly until the sauce thickens.

Cheese Sauce
• **SUITABLE FOR FREEZING**

1 cup white sauce
½ cup grated cheese

1. After making the white sauce, remove the saucepan from the heat and stir in the grated cheese.

Bechamel Sauce

• MAKES 1 CUP SAUCE • SUITABLE FOR FREEZING

1 carrot, chopped
1 onion, chopped
1 stalk celery, sliced
1 bay leaf
300 ml full-cream milk

1. Simmer the carrot, onion, celery and bay leaf in the milk for 30 minutes.
2. Strain; reserve the milk and make as for basic white sauce (see page 97) using the reserved milk instead of full-cream milk.

White, cheese and bechamel sauces are the bases for many recipes. They can be mixed with chicken, salmon or tuna and cooked pasta dishes. They can also be used in many vegetable dishes.

Basic Tomato Sauce

• MAKES 2 CUPS • SUITABLE FOR FREEZING

1 tablespoon olive oil
1 small onion, peeled and finely chopped
2 cloves garlic, finely sliced
1 small carrot, scraped and grated
400 g tin tomatoes or 500 g fresh, peeled tomatoes
½ teaspoon sugar
pepper
a pinch of salt
1 tablespoon finely chopped fresh basil

1. Heat the oil in a pan. Add the onion, garlic and carrot and cook until the onion is soft but not browned.

2. Add the tomatoes, coarsely chopped but not drained, the sugar, pepper and salt.

3. Partially cover the pan and simmer over a very low heat for about 40 minutes, stirring occasionally.

4. Add the fresh basil at the last minute.

This tomato sauce can be used as a foundation for many dishes. Turn it into different meals by adding mushrooms, eggplant, capsicum, chopped ham, canned tuna or browned minced beef.

It can be served over pasta or used for a sauce on a pizza.

Hoummos (chick pea dip)

This dip provides a complementary protein mixture, which is excellent for vegetarians and a great dip or spread for non-vegetarians. Hoummos also adds flavour to vegetable dishes.

Prepared hoummos is widely available from supermarkets, delis and specialty shops.

CHAPTER 12

Dried Beans, Peas and Lentils

Dried beans, peas and lentils all fall into the category of legumes or pulses. They are a wonderful addition to stews, casseroles, vegetables and soups. They are an excellent source of protein, especially when combined with foods made from grains such as bread, noodles and rice.

They are easy to mash and puree so are suitable for babies from 6 months onwards who are still learning how to deal with lumpy food. Always check instructions on packets of dried beans for soaking and pre-cooking. Dried red lentils do not need soaking or pre-cooking. If the thought of having to soak beans overnight and boil them for lengthy periods bothers you, pre-cooked tinned beans are a good alternative.

Always tip canned beans into a strainer and rinse them under running water to wash away any salt or additives.

Cheesy Baked Beans and Pumpkin
LUNCH OR DINNER
• 2 TODDLER SERVES • SUITABLE FOR BABIES 6–9 MONTHS

½ cup cooked pumpkin
½ cup canned baked beans
1 tablespoon grated cheese

1. Combine all the ingredients and heat gently.
2. Mash, blend or mouli (according to your baby's preference).
Add a little milk if a thinner consistency is desired.

Rice and Lentil Hotpot
LUNCH OR DINNER
• 2 TODDLER SERVES • SUITABLE FOR BABIES 6–9 MONTHS
• SUITABLE FOR FREEZING

1 tablespoon red lentils
1 tablespoon long-grain rice
1 small carrot, peeled and sliced
1 small stick celery, diced
1 small piece swede, chopped
400 g can tomatoes plus juice
1 clove garlic
1 tablespoon chopped fresh parsley

1. Place all the ingredients except the parsley in a small
saucepan and barely cover with water.
2. Cover and simmer gently for 30 minutes, adding just
enough liquid to keep the mixture from sticking to the
bottom of the pan, if necessary.
3. Drain and reserve the cooking liquid.
4. Blend the mixture with the chopped parsley, using the
cooking liquid to give the required consistency.

Lentil Soup with Pasta
LUNCH OR DINNER

• FAMILY SERVE • SUITABLE FOR BABIES 6–9 MONTHS
• SUITABLE FOR FREEZING (WITHOUT YOGHURT)

4 tablespoons olive oil
2 carrots, scraped and sliced
2 stalks celery, finely chopped
1 onion, peeled and sliced
400 g can tomatoes, chopped
½ cup red lentils
½ cup small pasta such as fafale (soup pasta) or risini (rice pasta)
1 litre homemade chicken or vegetable stock (see pages 60–61)
yoghurt, to serve

1. Heat the oil in a large pan and sauté the carrot, celery and onion for 5 minutes, or until the onion is soft.
2. Add the tomatoes, lentils and pasta.
3. Continue stirring for 2 minutes.
4. Add the stock. Bring to the boil and simmer over a low heat for about 45 minutes.
5. Blend until smooth. This will have to be done in batches.
6. Serve with a dollop of yoghurt.

CHAPTER 13

Soups

Soups are an excellent form of nourishment and babies can share family soups from 6 months onwards. If you are concerned about any strong or hot flavourings, add them after removing a baby portion. It is easier to feed babies thick soup. Thin broth can be thickened with rice cereal or ground rice.

Most soups freeze well although milk-based soups should not be boiled when reheating. You may prefer to add milk, cream or yoghurt during reheating.

See pages 59–62 for stock recipes and information.

Susan's Pick-Me-Up Chicken Noodle Soup
LUNCH OR DINNER
• FAMILY SERVE • SUITABLE FOR FREEZING • SUITABLE FOR BABIES 6–9 MONTHS

My friend Susan serves this once a week. If Isobel (a busy toddler) or Cressida (an even busier 4-year-old) get run down or have an attack of the sneezes and sniffles, Susan automatically makes up a big batch twice a week.

4 cups homemade chicken stock (see page 60)
½ vegetable stock cube (Massel brand)
125 g thin noodles
1½ cups chopped carrots
½ cup chopped celery
½ cup chopped broccoli (or green beans, peas, zucchini or parsley)
leftover chicken pieces, optional
½ cup chopped fresh parsley

I. Bring the chicken stock and halved stock cube to the boil in a large pan.
2. Add the noodles.
3. Add the carrots, celery and broccoli and any leftover chicken pieces, if used.
4. Simmer for 10 minutes. The noodles and vegetables absorb the goodness of the chicken stock. Add extra stock or water if more liquid is needed.
5. Blend or mouli a portion for your baby.

Potato and Leek Soup
LUNCH OR DINNER
• FAMILY SERVE

30 g butter
2 tablespoons vegetable oil
2 leeks, washed, trimmed and sliced
1 onion, peeled and chopped
2 large potatoes, peeled and chopped
600 ml homemade chicken stock (see page 60)
½ teaspoon ground nutmeg
ground black pepper
2 cups milk
finely chopped chives, to garnish

I. Heat the butter and oil in a heavy-based saucepan over low heat and cook the leeks and onion covered, stirring occasionally, for 10 minutes, or until softened.

2. Add the potatoes and continue cooking over a low heat, stirring from time to time to prevent sticking, until the potato starts to soften.

3. Add the stock, nutmeg and pepper and bring to the boil. Cover and simmer until the potato is cooked.

4. Remove from the heat. Blend the soup until smooth. This may have to be done in batches.

5. Return to the saucepan and add 2 cups milk. Reheat but do not boil.

6. Serve garnished with chives.

Orange Carrot Soup
LUNCH OR DINNER
• FAMILY SERVE • SUITABLE FOR FREEZING

1 kg carrots, scraped and chopped
1 onion, peeled and chopped
3½ cups homemade chicken stock (see page 60)
2 cups freshly squeezed orange juice

I. Cook the carrots and onion in the stock for approximately 20 minutes.

2. Transfer the vegies and a small amount of the stock to a blender and blend until smooth. (This may have to be done in batches.)

3. Return the pureed vegies to the saucepan. Add the orange juice and reheat.

4. Serve hot or chilled with a swirl of yoghurt.

Minestrone
LUNCH OR DINNER
• FAMILY SERVE • SUITABLE FOR FREEZING

2 tablespoons olive oil
1 onion, peeled and chopped
1 clove garlic, crushed
2 carrots, peeled and chopped
2 stalks celery, chopped
½ cup rindless bacon, chopped
2 cups homemade beef stock (see pages 61–62)
2 cups canned vegetable juice
2 cups water
1 tablespoon tomato paste
1 large potato, peeled and diced
¼ small cabbage, shredded
½ cup peas
400 g can three bean mix
2 teaspoons chopped fresh sage
2 teaspoons chopped fresh oregano
pepper
grated Parmesan cheese, to serve

1. Heat the oil in a large pan over a medium heat.
2. Add the onion, garlic, carrots, celery and bacon and cook until the onion is soft and transparent, about 5–10 minutes.
3. Add the stock, vegetable juice, water, tomato paste, potato, cabbage and peas. Cover and simmer over a low heat for about 40 minutes.
4. Add the bean mix, sage and oregano and continue to cook for a further 15–20 minutes. Add pepper to taste.
5. Serve with grated Parmesan cheese.

6. Mash, puree or mouli a portion for your baby, according to her preference.

Corn and Chicken Chowder
LUNCH OR DINNER
• FAMILY SERVE • SUITABLE FOR BABIES 6–9 MONTHS • SUITABLE FOR FREEZING

4 cups homemade chicken stock (see page 60)
1 cup minced lean chicken
310 g can creamed corn
1 large potato, diced
¼ cup chopped fresh parsley

1. Place the stock, chicken, corn and potato in a large pan. Cover and bring to the boil, then reduce the heat and simmer for 20–30 minutes.
2. Stir in the parsley and allow to cool slightly.
3. Blend until smooth.

Jann's Pumpkin Soup
LUNCH OR DINNER
• FAMILY SERVE • SUITABLE FOR FREEZING

2 tablespoons butter
2 onions, finely chopped
250 g tomatoes, peeled and chopped
500 g pumpkin, diced
1 litre homemade chicken stock (see page 60)
a pinch of salt
freshly ground black pepper
fresh cream (optional)
2 tablespoons chopped fresh basil

1. Melt the butter in a heavy-based saucepan over a

medium heat. Add the onions and cook until soft, about 5 minutes.

2. Add the tomatoes and cook for 10 minutes.

3. Add the pumpkin and chicken stock and bring to the boil.

4. Cover and simmer gently for about 30 minutes or until the pumpkin is soft. Remove from the heat. Add salt and pepper to taste and mix to a puree.

5. Reheat the puree and serve with a dollop of cream and a sprinkle of finely chopped basil.

6. Omit the cream for your baby.

Lamb and Vegetable Soup
LUNCH OR DINNER

• **FAMILY SERVE** • **SUITABLE FOR BABIES 6–9 MONTHS** • **SUITABLE FOR FREEZING**

1 lamb shank
1 stalk celery, sliced
1 carrot, chopped
1 onion, peeled and chopped
¼ cup pearl barley
¼ cup split peas
1 litre homemade vegetable stock (see page 61)

1. Place all the ingredients in a large pan. Cover and bring to the boil. Simmer gently until the meat easily comes off the bone, about 1½ hours.

2. Remove all the meat from the shank and return to the soup mixture. Discard the bone.

3. Blend or mouli the soup until smooth. This may need to be done in batches.

CHAPTER 14

Meat and Chicken

Meat and chicken are an important source of protein, iron and zinc, as well as a range of vitamins.

Not eating meat is fine for babies and toddlers when dairy products are included and suitable alternatives for meat are used. If you eat very little meat yourself but are not strictly vegetarian, think about giving your baby or toddler meat once or twice a week (presuming, of course, that she likes it) as including meat and chicken adds to the variety of food available to her. Meat is also a good way for her to get an easily absorbed form of iron.

Generally, meat and chicken have to be minced for babies, as most of them tend to gag a lot on lumpy meat until they are over 12 months. However, slices of moist medium-rare meat cut into fingers is good to give as finger food as soon as your baby is interested in picking up food herself (6–12 months). The strips of meat usually get chewed and sucked on then discarded.

The easiest way to give meat to babies in the first year is combined with a hotpot or stew then put through a mouli or blender. This can be prepared especially for your baby (lean minced beef or lamb is the easiest meat to use for this) or she can have a portion of a family dish blended to the consistency she likes best.

Basic Baby Beef Stew
LUNCH OR DINNER
• 2–3 BABY SERVES • SUITABLE FOR BABIES 6–9 MONTHS
• SUITABLE FOR FREEZING

This forms the basis for a main meal. Many babies will happily eat variations of this most days.

1 small potato
1 small carrot
1 small piece pumpkin
3 broccoli or cauliflower florets
homemade beef stock (see pages 61–62) or water, to cover
1 teaspoon tomato paste
1 small clove garlic, crushed
100 g minced lean beef
1 teaspoon olive oil
1 teaspoon chopped fresh parsley
grated cheese

1. Peel and cut the potato, carrot and pumpkin into chunks.
2. Place in a saucepan with the broccoli and cover with the beef stock or water.
3. Stir in the tomato paste.
4. Lightly fry the minced beef and garlic in the oil in a non-stick frying pan, over medium to high heat, until the beef is just brown.
5. Add the beef and garlic to the saucepan.
6. Cover and simmer until the vegetables are tender. Add parsley.

7. Put through a mouli or blender.

8. Stir in the grated cheese while still hot.

VARIATIONS
- Any vegetable combinations can be used – try spinach, cabbage, zucchini, mushrooms, peas or green beans.
- Try adding herbs and flavourings such as basil, oregano or paprika.

Basic Meat Casserole
LUNCH OR DINNER
• FAMILY SERVE (SERVES 4) • SUITABLE FOR BABIES 6–9 MONTHS
• SUITABLE FOR FREEZING

1 tablespoon vegetable oil

1 small onion, peeled and sliced

1 carrot, peeled and sliced

500 g lean beef, trimmed and cut into small chunks (use gravy beef, blade or chuck)

1 piece pumpkin, peeled and chopped

400 g can tomatoes

1 cup homemade beef stock (see pages 61–62)

2 tablespoons chopped fresh parsley

1 bay leaf

pepper

1. Heat the oil in a frying pan and fry the onion and carrot until soft. Add the beef chunks and cook until browned.

2. Transfer the beef, onions and carrot to a heavy-based pan and stir in all the other ingredients.

3. Cover and simmer for 1½ hours, adding more stock or water if required, or until the beef is tender.

4. Blend or mouli, according to what your baby likes best.

VARIATIONS
- Vary this dish by changing the vegetables. Try sweet potato, zucchini, eggplant or broccoli.
- Add herbs such as basil, marjoram or oregano.
- Add barley and mushrooms.

Bokmakierie Robertson's Father's Scottish Stew
LUNCH OR DINNER
• FAMILY MEAL • SUITABLE FOR BABIES 6–9 MONTHS
• SUITABLE FOR FREEZING

This recipe makes an enormous pot of stew that lasts all week for a small family. Bokmakierie has half a cup minced up with lots of spinach and loves it.

Stew is economical, easy to make and almost impossible to spoil in the cooking. It is surprising how tender and flavoursome cheap gravy beef can be.

750 g boneless gravy beef, cubed
2 tablespoons vegetable oil
2 brown onions, peeled and chopped
2 teaspoons plain flour
10 cups water
180 g can tomato paste
1 cup instant dried peas
8 hefty cloves garlic, sliced – do not use a garlic press
1 turnip, chopped
2 carrots, sliced
4 potatoes, chopped
250 g red lentils or 125 g barley
1 tablespoon fresh chopped tarragon
1 large bay leaf

½ teaspoon vegetable salt
2 tablespoons rolled oats
1 bunch spinach, well washed

1. Use a sharp chopping knife to trim the beef and scissors to cut it into small 15 mm blocks — not strips.

2. Heat the oil in a large heavy-based pan over a medium heat. Add the beef and onions and cook until the beef is browned.

3. Reduce heat and sprinkle the flour over the beef and stir through. Add water and gradually stir to loosen pan sediment.

4. Add the remaining ingredients, apart from the spinach, and stir well.

5. Ingredients should be almost covered with water, so add more if necessary.

6. Simmer covered over a low heat for 2–3 hours, stirring occasionally to prevent sticking and adding more water if necessary.

TO SERVE

Finely slice or chop the raw spinach, putting a good amount in each deep bowl. Ladle piping hot stew over the greens. Wait about 5 minutes before serving. The heat of the stew will lightly cook the spinach.

May be eaten at once but is best kept frozen in small containers until required. Blend, mash or mouli portions for baby.

IMPORTANT

When reheating, add extra water — the stew seems to become thicker during storage.

VARIATIONS

- For different meals add one or more of the following to the night's stew:

  1 tablespoon of peanut butter (for babies over 12 months)

  1 teaspoon wholegrain prepared mustard

  1 tablespoon concentrated pesto sauce

- Sprinkle grated cheese over the stew.

Creamed Brains
LUNCH OR DINNER

• 4 BABY SERVES • SUITABLE FOR BABIES 6–9 MONTHS

• SUITABLE FOR FREEZING

2 potatoes, peeled, boiled and chopped
1 set brains, soaked for 30 minutes in cold water to cover with
a squeeze of lemon juice
2 tablespoons milk
1 tablespoon chopped fresh parsley
grated cheese, to sprinkle

1. Wash the brains and remove the skin. Place in a small saucepan. Barely cover with water. Simmer gently until cooked through, about 5–8 minutes. Drain well.

2. Process or blend the potatoes, brains, milk and parsley together until smooth.

3. Serve sprinkled with a little grated cheese.

Liver with Apples
LUNCH OR DINNER

• 4–5 BABY SERVES OR 2 TODDLER SERVES

• SUITABLE FOR BABIES 6–9 MONTHS • SUITABLE FOR FREEZING

1 tablespoon olive oil
1 tablespoon butter
250 g chicken livers, trimmed and chopped
1 large apple, peeled and sliced
1 onion, peeled and chopped
½ cup apple juice

1. Heat the oil and butter in a frying pan.
2. Add the livers, apple and onion and cook until the onion is soft and golden brown.
3. Add the apple juice and simmer, stirring, until the liquid reduces, about 3–5 minutes.
4. Mash, blend or mouli according to your baby's preference. Serve with mashed potato, rice or pasta.

Liver Casserole
LUNCH OR DINNER

• 4–5 BABY SERVES OR 2 TODDLER SERVES • SUITABLE FOR BABIES 6–9 MONTHS

• SUITABLE FOR FREEZING

2 tablespoons olive oil
1 red or white onion, peeled and chopped
1 large carrot, peeled and chopped
250 g calf's liver, trimmed and thinly sliced
1 potato, peeled and chopped
2 tomatoes, skinned, seeded and chopped
2 tablespoons chopped fresh parsley
½ cup water, if needed

1. Heat the oil in a heavy-based frying pan.
2. Sauté the onion, carrot and liver until the onion is soft and golden.
3. Add the tomatoes, potato, parsley and water.
4. Cover and simmer over a low heat for 5–10 minutes, or until the liver is cooked through.
5. Mash, blend or mouli according to your baby's preference.

Simple Bolognaise
LUNCH OR DINNER
• FAMILY SERVE • MEAT SAUCE SUITABLE FOR FREEZING

2 tablespoons olive oil
1 onion, peeled and sliced
1 clove garlic, crushed
½ green capsicum, chopped
500 g finely minced lean beef
1 carrot, scraped and grated
2 mushrooms, peeled and chopped
2 tablespoons tomato paste
400 g can tomatoes, chopped
½ cup homemade beef stock (see pages 61–62)
2 teaspoons chopped fresh oregano
375 g pasta of choice, freshly cooked
grated Parmesan cheese, to serve

1. Heat the oil in a large heavy-based frying pan and sauté the onion, garlic and capsicum until the onion becomes soft and translucent. Do not let the garlic burn.
2. Add the minced beef, breaking it up with a wooden spoon as it cooks until it becomes brown and crumbled.
3. Add the carrot and mushrooms and cook for 1 minute.

4. Stir in the tomato paste, tomatoes, stock and oregano. Bring to the boil then reduce the heat, cover and simmer, stirring occasionally, for 30 minutes.

5. Toss the sauce through the hot freshly cooked pasta.

6. Sprinkle with grated Parmesan cheese.

7. Blend or mouli a portion for your baby. (See page 128 for a guide to blending pasta for babies.)

Shepherd's Pie
LUNCH OR DINNER
• FAMILY SERVE • SUITABLE FOR FREEZING

1 tablespoon vegetable oil

1 onion, peeled and chopped

500 g finely minced lean beef

½ cup grated cabbage

½ cup grated carrot

1 zucchini, finely chopped

2 tablespoons plain flour

1 cup water or homemade beef stock (see pages 61–62)

2 tablespoons chopped fresh parsley

4 potatoes, peeled

¼ cup milk

15 g butter

½ cup grated cheese

¼ cup dry breadcrumbs

1. Preheat the oven to 180°C.

2. Heat the oil in a large frying pan and sauté the onion gently until it becomes soft and translucent.

3. Add the minced beef, breaking it up with a wooden spoon as it cooks over medium to high heat until it becomes brown and crumbled.

4. Add the cabbage, carrot and zucchini and stir for about 5 minutes.

5. Stir in the flour and cook, stirring, for 1 minute.

6. Add the water and parsley and bring to the boil.

7. Simmer, stirring, for about 5 minutes, or until the mixture thickens.

8. Cover and simmer gently for 30 minutes.

9. Boil, drain and mash the potatoes until smooth. Beat in the milk and butter.

10. Spoon the beef mixture into a deep pie dish. Layer the mashed potato over the top.

11. Mix together the cheese and breadcrumbs and sprinkle over the potato.

12. Bake for 15–20 minutes or until the top is golden.

13. Puree, mouli or mash a portion for baby.

Chicken Puree
LUNCH OR DINNER
• 4 BABY SERVES • SUITABLE FOR BABIES 6–9 MONTHS

125 g skinless chicken breast fillet, chopped
½ cup homemade chicken stock (see page 60)
1 tablespoon chopped fresh parsley
1 tablespoon natural yoghurt

1. Simmer the chicken gently in the stock in a tightly covered pan until cooked through.

2. Place the chicken in a food processor or blender with the parsley and yoghurt, using a little of the cooking liquid if necessary. Blend until smooth.

VARIATION

- This dish can also be made using cooked chicken. Simply puree with a little milk for extra fluid if necessary.

Basic Chicken Casserole
LUNCH OR DINNER
• 4 BABY SERVES OR 2 TODDLER SERVES • SUITABLE FOR BABIES 6–9 MONTHS

2 tablespoons vegetable oil
125 g skinless chicken breast fillet, sliced
1 potato, chopped
1 carrot, sliced
1 piece pumpkin, peeled and chopped
1 stalk celery, chopped
1 tomato, chopped
1 clove garlic, crushed
1 teaspoon chopped fresh sage
1 tablespoon tomato paste
2 tablespoons chopped fresh parsley
1 cup homemade chicken stock (see page 60)

1. Preheat the oven to 180°C.
2. Heat the oil in a large pan over a medium heat.
3. Add the chicken and potato, carrot, pumpkin and celery and sauté until browned.
4. Add the tomato, garlic, sage, tomato paste, parsley and stock. Stir well.
5. Transfer the mixture into a casserole dish. Cover and bake for 1 hour.
6. Blend or mouli according to your baby's preference.

CHAPTER 15

Fish

Fish is an important part of a healthy diet. It contains a special fat that enhances the development of the brain, eye and blood vessels. Most babies can tolerate fish after 6 months of age; however, fish is one of the foods more commonly associated with intolerance or allergy. If there is a history of problems in your family, delay introducing fish until after the first year.

An extreme reaction to fish is unusual. Minor reactions are things like sudden vomiting, a rash (either around the mouth or over the body) or swelling of the lips. If these symptoms occur, and you suspect fish, wait a month before trying it again.

Fresh, frozen or canned fish are all suitable. When buying fresh fish, select boneless fillets of white fish (for example, ling or ocean perch). Frozen fillets are available in supermarkets, but check what coating is used as some are quite spicy hot. Remember, canned fish is available in spring water, an alternative to oil.

Any of the fish dishes following can be used as family dishes by increasing the size and number of fish fillets. Serve with vegies, rice or salad.

Baked Fish
LUNCH OR DINNER
• 1–2 BABY SERVES • SUITABLE FOR BABIES 6–9 MONTHS

1 fillet of white fish, about 150 g
½ lemon
a little butter

1. Preheat the oven to 180°C.
2. Squeeze a little lemon juice over the fillet of fish, dot with a little butter and wrap in aluminium foil.
3. Bake for about 10 minutes. Fish is cooked when it is soft and can be flaked easily.

TO MICROWAVE
1. Put the fish in a microwave-safe dish.
2. Squeeze lemon juice over and dot with butter.
3. Cover and cook in the microwave oven on high setting for about 2 minutes.
4. Fish is cooked when it is soft and can be flaked easily.

The fillets may also be poached or steamed until soft and flaky, then mashed or pureed with a little milk and some cooked vegetables, such as potato, carrot and broccoli.

Poached Fish
LUNCH OR DINNER
• 1–2 BABY SERVES • SUITABLE FOR BABIES 6–9 MONTHS

½ cup milk
1 fillet of white fish, about 150 g
a little butter

1. Place the milk, fish and a little butter in a small

heavy-based frying pan. Cover and simmer very gently until the fish is cooked, about 5–10 minutes.

Steamed Fish
LUNCH OR DINNER
• 1–2 BABY SERVES • SUITABLE FOR BABIES 6–9 MONTHS

1 fillet of white fish, about 150 g
½ lemon
a little butter
chopped fresh parsley

I. Place the fillet of fish on a heat-proof plate. Squeeze a little lemon juice over and dot with a little butter.
2. Place over a pan of boiling water or in a steamer over boiling water. Cover and cook for 10 minutes or until the fish is cooked.

Fish Pie
LUNCH OR DINNER
• FAMILY SERVE

350 g fillet of white fish, baked, poached or steamed – drained and flaked and cooking liquid reserved
½ cup basic white sauce (see page 97)
2 tablespoons grated Cheddar cheese
1 tablespoon chopped fresh parsley
1 hard-boiled egg, chopped
juice of ½ lemon
2 potatoes, cooked
½ cup milk
2 teaspoons butter

I. Preheat the oven to 180°C. Cook the fish as directed.

2. Warm the white sauce gently and add the flaked fish and liquid.

3. Stir through and cook gently, stirring constantly, until warmed through.

4. Add the cheese and stir until the cheese has melted into the sauce.

5. Stir in the parsley, chopped eggs and lemon juice.

6. Pour the fish mixture into a greased pie dish.

7. Mash the potato with milk and butter until smooth.

8. Spread over the mixture. Bake for 15–20 minutes.

9. Mash, puree or mouli, according to your baby's preference.

CHAPTER 16

Eggs

Eggs are ideal for babies as they can be easily cooked and served in small quantities. They are especially useful as a quick substitute when the family meal is unsuitable.

Egg is another one of the foods more commonly associated with intolerance or allergy. If there is a history of problems in your family, delay introducing egg until the second year.

For most babies, egg yolk may be commenced any time after 9 months. Soft-boil an egg and try giving some yolk off a spoon or dip a finger of toast or bread into the yolk and let your baby suck it. A hard-boiled yolk can be grated into her vegies at lunch or dinner.

The whole egg can be given at 12 months. Minor reactions to egg whites are things like mild swelling of the lips and/or a sudden appearance of a red rash around the mouth. Sudden vomiting can also be a sign of a problem with egg.

If any of these things happen, leave eggs until your baby is over 12 months. Life-threatening reactions (see pages 16–17) to eggs are rare but seem to be increasing.

Whole egg cooked in custards and other dishes should be safe for non-allergic babies after 9 months.

Poached Egg
BREAKFAST, LUNCH OR DINNER

water
1 teaspoon butter
1 egg

1. Fill a small saucepan three-quarters full of water.
2. Add the butter.
3. Bring water to the boil.
4. Crack an egg into a cup. Stir the boiling water with a balloon whisk and slide the egg into it.
5. Reduce the heat so that the water simmers.
6. Poach for 1–2 minutes.
7. Lift out with a slotted spoon.

Boiled Egg
BREAKFAST, LUNCH OR DINNER

1 egg
water

1. Place the egg in a saucepan and cover with water.
2. Bring the water to boiling point and remove from the stove.
3. Allow to stand for 3–4 minutes for soft, 5–6 minutes for medium or 8–10 minutes for hard-boiled.
4. Serve soft- and medium-boiled eggs with fingers of buttered toast or 'soldiers'.

Scrambled Egg
BREAKFAST, LUNCH OR DINNER

1 teaspoon butter
2 eggs, lightly beaten
salt and ground pepper

1. Melt the butter in a small pan until sizzling but not brown.
2. Pour the eggs into the pan and stir constantly with a wooden spoon, over a low heat, until just thickened.
3. Season the beaten egg with salt and pepper to taste.

VARIATIONS
• Add the following to the beaten egg, separately or in combinations:

    ½ chopped, peeled tomato
    I tablespoon grated Cheddar cheese
    I tablespoon chopped parsley

Creamy Egg Mornay
BREAKFAST, LUNCH OR DINNER
• 1 BABY SERVE

1 tablespoon grated Cheddar cheese
2 teaspoons rice cereal or ground rice
¼ cup hot milk
1 hard-boiled egg

1. Stir the cheese and baby cereal into the hot milk in a saucepan over a medium heat until thickened.
2. Mash or chop the egg, according to the consistency your baby likes best, and add it to the sauce.

Sylvia's Tomato and Poached Egg
BREAKFAST, LUNCH OR DINNER
• 1 BABY OR 1 TODDLER SERVE

Sylvia is one of my mother's best friends. I asked her for a recipe and was delighted to get this one, especially as it contains salt and sugar, nowadays politically very incorrect. I also love the comment about 'the usual vegies' — why do we search today for endless variation?

1 tomato, peeled and sliced
a pinch each of salt and sugar
1 egg

1. Put the tomato in a small saucepan with the salt and sugar and cook gently until soft.
2. Break in the egg and poach until set.

An easy and tasty lunch for young children. Any other lunch was just the usual vegies.

Thin Chinese Omelette
SNACK/FINGER FOOD
• 1 BABY OR 1 TODDLER SERVE

1 egg, lightly beaten
1 teaspoon butter or sesame oil

1. Heat a small frying pan until the base is quite hot.
2. Melt the butter or sesame oil in the pan over a medium heat.
3. Pour the beaten egg into the pan until the mixture covers the base.
4. Let cook through for 1–2 minutes.
5. Slide out of the pan.
6. Roll up and thinly slice.

CHAPTER 17

Pasta and Rice

Pasta

Pasta is satisfying and economical and babies and toddlers often love it. Babies can eat pasta dishes from the age of 6 months, but many babies between 6 and 12 months still need their food ground up. As some pasta dishes are difficult to put through a blender or a mouli, you may be a little restricted until your baby can handle lumpier food (often after 12 months).

To successfully blend pasta dishes, you need to pick recipes that have plenty of sauce. Small, thin or fine pasta or noodles will be easier to blend. You can add some milk or water to assist in the process.

To Cook Pasta

As a general rule, pasta will double its bulk when cooked.

Cook the pasta in plenty of boiling water with a little oil or butter added to prevent sticking. Be sure the water is really boiling before adding the pasta. Do not overcook it. The time depends on the type and size of the pasta. You will find recommended times given on the packet. Once cooked, drain pasta well, using a colander.

If you look around the shelves in the supermarket you will find a big selection of pasta in different shapes and sizes. One of the most common is spaghetti, which is the thickest stick pasta. Others are vermicelli, spaghettini and angel hair, which are finer.

Flat ribbon pasta, such as fettuccine and tagliatelle, comes in different widths. Lasagne is the widest.

Small pasta varieties such as macaroni, farfalle, risini, alphabet pasta or fine noodles are good to use for babies.

Simple Macaroni Cheese
LUNCH OR DINNER
• FAMILY SERVE • SUITABLE FOR BABIES 6–9 MONTHS

2 tablespoons butter
2 tablespoons plain flour
1 cup warm milk
1 cup homemade vegetable or chicken stock (see pages 60–61)
1 cup grated Cheddar cheese
4 cups cooked macaroni
1 tablespoon dry breadcrumbs
extra 10 g butter, for topping

1. Preheat the oven to 200°C.
2. Melt the butter in a saucepan over a low heat. Stir in the flour and cook for 1 minute, stirring constantly with a wooden spoon.
3. Gradually add the milk, stirring constantly.
4. Gradually add the stock and stir in two-thirds of the cheese.
5. Continue cooking over a low heat for a further 3 minutes.
6. Combine the macaroni with the sauce. Place into a greased baking dish. Sprinkle over the remaining cheese and breadcrumbs and dot with butter.

7. Bake for 15–20 minutes.

8. Blend or mouli a portion for your baby, adding more milk or stock if necessary.

VARIATION

*   Add ½ cup chopped cooked ham and 1 cup chopped tomato, shredded spinach or grated carrot and 1 beaten egg to the mixture before baking.

Rice

Rice is a great-tasting, healthy basis for many meals. As with pasta, to successfully blend or mouli rice for babies you need plenty of liquid – add some stock, water or milk to assist in the process if necessary.

Rice can be a dish on its own, hot or cold, served as an accompaniment to meat and fish instead of potatoes or added to soups, stews, casseroles and stir-fries.

Brown rice gives a nuttier flavour, more fibre and a little more iron. Long-grain rice is good for savoury dishes and salads. Short-grain rice is good for soups and puddings. Arborio is a plump short-grain rice that is ideal for risotto.

Rice cooks better by the absorption method.

Other recipes using pasta and rice are included in all sections of the book.

Boiled Rice

2 cups water
1 cup rice

1. Bring 2 cups of water to the boil in a heavy-based pan.

2. Add 1 cup of raw rice, cover and cook for 25 minutes

for white rice, or 40 minutes for brown rice, until all liquid is absorbed.

Jann's Easy Rice Pudding
LUNCH OR DINNER

• 2–4 BABY SERVES

• SUITABLE FOR BABIES 6–9 MONTHS WHO DON'T MIND LUMPS

1 cup cooked rice
1 cup milk, warmed
a few drops vanilla flavouring essence
1 tablespoon sugar

1. Combine all the ingredients.
2. Cook very gently for 10 minutes until the rice is heated through.

Simple Chicken Risotto
LUNCH OR DINNER

• FAMILY SERVE • SUITABLE FOR BABIES 6–9 MONTHS

• SUITABLE FOR FREEZING

1 tablespoon vegetable oil
1 small onion, peeled and finely chopped
1 clove garlic, crushed
300 g minced lean chicken
2 mushrooms, brushed and thinly sliced
1 large tomato, peeled, seeded and chopped
1 stick celery, diced
1 tablespoon chopped fresh mint
1 tablespoon chopped fresh parsley
1 cup arborio rice
3 cups homemade chicken stock (see page 60)

1. Heat the oil in a large heavy-based pan. Add the onion and garlic and cook for a few minutes, stirring over a medium heat.

2. Add the minced chicken and brown, stirring occasionally, for a few minutes.

3. Add the mushrooms, tomato, celery, mint and parsley. Stir well and cook for 1 minute.

4. Stir in the rice, then add the stock. Bring to the boil, then cover and simmer for about 30 minutes, stirring occasionally to prevent sticking, or until the liquid is absorbed and the rice tender. Add extra liquid if necessary.

5. Blend or mouli a portion for your baby.

CHAPTER 18

Finger Food

Finger food is food babies can pick up and eat themselves. Around 9 months is an ideal time to start finger food because most babies are very interested in putting everything in their mouths around this time and especially like experimenting with food. Note, however, that some babies are interested before 9 months, and others not until 12 months.

Finger food works better when your baby can sit for a reasonable time in a high chair – this happens anytime between 6 and 9 months.

As babies have to learn how much to bite off and how to get the food down, there may be some interesting moments when your baby gags and frightens the life out of you. Or times when food gets stored up on her palate and you have to retrieve it. Finger food also gets rubbed in the hair, pushed into ears and thrown around the room; however, learning to eat finger food is part of progressing to family food.

The best time for finger food is following the pureed part of the meal or between meals, at morning and afternoon tea times. Finger food does not have to be given at every mealtime or even every day at this age, unless your baby is really taken

ses it if it's not around. Give finger food when
me to supervise and are not rushing out the

piece of food on the tray of the high chair. If it gets eaten, put some more down. If it all starts to become a game, finish up. Limit the time to eat the finger food to about ten minutes or less.

Many babies aged between 6 and 9 months will start eating finger food reasonably efficiently; however, just as many won't show any inclination to eat finger food until they are older – nearer to 12 months. If your baby shows no interest or just squashes the food up and sticks it in her ear or up her nose, just offer finger food every so often until she gets the idea.

As babies move towards 12 months and into the toddler years, eating with their fingers is the best way for them to learn to feed themselves. A greater variety of food can be offered and many babies will be eating some or all of their meals with their fingers.

Remember, the arrival of teeth has nothing to do with the best time to start finger foods. Babies' gums are hard and sharp and chew up food well.

First Finger Foods

- Rusks
- Muffins
- Felafel
- Bone-free flakes of cooked fish
- Hard-boiled egg, sliced (one slice at a time)
- Scrambled egg
- Sandwiches
- Bread and toast fingers

- Grilled tomato and cheese on toast
- Avocado on toast
- Cruskets
- Cooked pasta
- Slices of cooked meat and chicken (may be chewed and chewed then spat out – that's okay)
- Grilled bacon rashers, well-drained
- Little mounds of grated cheese, carrot and apple (very little and offer one mound at a time)
- Cheese sticks
- Smooth lamb cutlet bone (left over from adult meal)
- Fingers of soft ripe fruit – rockmelon, mango, peach, pear, watermelon, kiwi fruit, seedless grapes
- Partially steamed or microwaved vegetables cut into strips – potato, carrot, pumpkin, green beans, zucchini
- Rice cakes

Look for other finger food ideas in Part Four
- Basic Frittata
- Polenta with Tomato Sauce
- Fish Croquettes
- Spicy Chicken Wings
- Kate's Little Meatballs
- Pizzas
- The Barker Tacos
- Strips of crumbed chicken breast or veal fillets
- Stir-fry meals

THE THIRD STAGE: TODDLERS AND BEYOND

CHAPTER 19

The Mighty Toddler

Once babies reach 12 months of age they are called toddlers. Babies under 12 months can eat many of these recipes and, of course, many of the recipes in Part Three are also suitable for toddlers.

Many of the recipes in this section are family recipes that toddlers can share, or toddler recipes that families can share. Toddlers often like to eat with their fingers, so there are plenty of ideas for finger food.

'Toddlerhood' refers to the stage of development that follows the baby era. It is a time of tremendous development, when babies discover they are able to use their minds and bodies and make things happen.

Here are some typical toddler characteristics.

Toddlers are:
- Imaginative, energetic, busy.
- Keen to explore and very curious.
- Easily frustrated and need lots of attention (especially lots of kisses and hugs).
- Determined and often independent.
- Very particular and choosy, with distinct likes and dislikes.

And they have:

- Very short attention spans and memories (apart from times when their memories are like an elephant's and their attention will not waver from the chocolates at the supermarket check-out).
- A much slower growth rate, and many toddlers have a much reduced appetite once they are past the first year.

Fussy toddler eating is the bane of many parents' lives. If this is happening to you, try to see it more as a phase of normal development rather than what's on the plate.

Here are some tips:

- As a general rule, healthy toddlers *will* eat when they are hungry. By the time they have consumed endless quantities of milk, juice and water and many little snacks, toddlers are often not really hungry at mealtimes. Cut down on fluids, stop the bottles and avoid fluids one hour before meals. Resist the temptation to replace meals with bottles of milk. If healthy snacking helps you both through the day, that's fine. But meals are likely to be a non-event.
- Many toddlers will only eat one good meal every day or two and pick at bits and pieces the rest of the time. Try not to expect your toddler to eat the way you do yet.
- Limit mealtimes to 15–20 minutes, snacks to ten minutes.
- Try to look at the big picture rather than the day-to-day issues. For most toddlers this is only a phase that they pass through. As long as the family diet is well balanced and your toddler has access to a variety of healthy foods, she will be fine.

Parents with non-eating toddlers become a little weary when they are constantly told 'don't worry, it's normal' by cheerful health professionals. Occasionally there is an underlying problem that needs help.

When to Worry

- If your toddler is constantly unhappy, lethargic and uninterested in the world around her. Or if she is doing what you consider to be a lot of strange poo.
- If she loses weight or does not gain weight over a period of a few months, which cannot be explained by an acute illness (such as gastroenteritis).
- If there are ongoing social or emotional family problems you can't resolve that may be affecting your toddler's appetite.

If any of the above apply to your toddler, seek help from your early childhood nurse, GP or paediatrician.

Toddlers in the Kitchen (eeek)

Involving toddlers in safe food activities helps them discover more about food than just what is presented to them at mealtimes.

Here are some ideas:
- Helping pack groceries away.
- Peeling bananas and adding to a smoothie.
- Spooning things out of packets.
- Counting (eggs, spoons and so on).
- Holding jugs and bowls while you mix.
- Mixing while you hold jugs and bowls.
- Remembering ingredients for familiar recipes.
- Licking cake bowls.

Constipation (hard poo)

'Constipation' refers to hard poo that a toddler has difficulty passing – not how often she goes. If she only goes every three days and it's soft, that's fine. If she goes three times a day and it's a little hard dry ball and she's distressed, it's constipation.

Toddlers often get temporarily constipated and it can be very upsetting for everyone. A few general guidelines follow.

- Fluids help babies and toddlers more than bulky food when they are constipated, so give extra water or juice (not milk) or add more fluid to meals when possible. Prune juice is excellent – dilute with a little water.
- A breakfast of porridge, Weet-Bix, Bran Bix, or Vita Brits with warm milk, undiluted prune juice and brown sugar helps (if your toddler will eat it, of course).
- Paw-paw is excellent. Serve mashed with freshly squeezed orange juice and a little sugar.

Most temporary constipation in toddlers can be helped by simple dietary measures, but sometimes it becomes chronic and needs other treatments such as the use of oral lubricants or mild aperients. If you are worried, see your GP.

Diarrhoea (loose poo)

- Diarrhoea can be caused by an infection (gastroenteritis), by food or medication, by an underlying medical problem (rare) or by a toddler's normal metabolism (toddler diarrhoea).
- Mild infectious diarrhoea is treated by giving toddlers clear fluids for 24 hours, then introducing them back to their normal diet over the next two days. If you are unsure of what to do or if your toddler is vomiting as well as having diarrhoea, seek medical advice immediately as toddlers can become dehydrated very quickly.
- If you think something in your toddler's diet is causing diarrhoea, obviously stop the food. If the diarrhoea is caused by medication, let your GP know.
- When diarrhoea is caused by a medical problem, the

toddler does not thrive and has no energy. These toddlers need special care from an appropriate health professional.

• Toddler diarrhoea is very common. The toddler often eats like a bird, drinks excessively and poos like an elephant many times a day. She is full of energy and thrives (while her mother and father nearly expire from the nappy changes). At this time of her life the food moves through her bowel faster than normal. Try to cut down on the fluids and as much as possible 'bulk' up her diet (rice and pasta) and make sure you include full-fat dairy products. A diet of fruit juice, fruit and vegies and no fat exacerbates toddler diarrhoea. Toddler diarrhoea usually slows down sometime between ages 2 and 3.

TODDLER BASIC DIET

- A guide to follow after 12 months.
- Formula in bottles can be replaced by full-fat cow's milk between 9 and 12 months.
- Two bottles of milk (180 ml) a day is all that's needed. Use a cup for fluids during the day.
- One cup of juice a day drunk in one sitting. No juice is even better. Offer water.
- 'Cup' means a straw or spout cup (whichever suits your toddler).

4.30–6 a.m (how uncivilised):
breastfeed or bottle feed (hopefully back to sleep)

Some babies/toddlers continue early-morning waking into the second year. Once they start sleeping longer, this early-morning feed stops. Bottles aren't needed past 12 months. Breastfeeding continues for as long as you are both happy to do so.

BREAKFAST 7– 9 a.m.

Eggs boiled, poached or scrambled

Thin Chinese Omelette

Emmanuel's Bread Dipped in Egg

Note: It is fine for toddlers to have an egg a day.

Cup of milk or water

Muffin, crumpet or bagel

The usual cereal/porridge

or Grilled cheese, avocado, ham, tomato or baked beans on toast

or Adam's Yoghurt

or Sarah's Breakfast Smoothie

MORNING TEA 10–11 a.m.
Snack and cup of milk or water and snack:
Fresh fruit, dried fruit, small sandwich, scone, pikelet, tomato, cucumber, cheese slice, cracker biscuit

LUNCH 12–1:30 p.m.

The 'main' meal can be now or in the evening.

Darcy's Pasta, Couscous or Rice

Sandwiches

Basic Frittata	Avocado/Tomato/Lentil Salad	**or** Jaffles
Fish Croquettes	Sarah and Miriam's Tuna Salad	**or** Basic Salad
Pizza	Polenta with Tomato Sauce	**or** Kate's Favourite Fruit
Salad		

Cup of milk or water (or a breastfeed or bottle feed)

AFTERNOON TEA 3–4 p.m.

Cup of milk or water and snack:
Muffin, slice of zucchini or raisin loaf, vegetable sticks, fresh fruit, fruit juice iceblock, frozen yoghurt, pikelet

DINNER (family food) 5–7 p.m.

Shepherd's Pie	Savoury Rice Loaf	Crumbed Veal or Chicken Fillet
Stir-Fry Chicken and Rice	Steamed Fish	The Barker Tacos
Chicken and Pasta Bake	Meatloaf in a Hurry	Noodle and Vegie Stir-fry
Fish Fingers		

All of the above with steamed vegies, rice or salad.

Fresh fruit on its own or with yoghurt, junket or custard/Grandma Dot's Bread Pudding/Chocolate Pudding with Mashed Pear

Cup of milk or water (or a breastfeed or bottle feed)

Despite your best intentions you may find your toddler only wants the same old thing day in and day out. Accept her limited tastes at this time in her life. Offer new things regularly, but try not to get frustrated if they are refused. Research shows that toddlers sometimes need to be offered the same food twenty or more times before they will accept it.

CHAPTER 20

Breakfast Ideas

Cereal or porridge is the main breakfast ingredient. Look for good-quality cereal and avoid the highly sugared, chocolate-flavoured variety. If your toddler never eats it, she'll never know it exists.

Combine cereal or porridge with fresh or cooked fruit and milk. A little sugar is fine, but if you'd rather not use any, don't.

Check out the recipes in Chapter 9 for other ideas with cereal.

Not all toddlers will eat cereal and, while useful and convenient, it's certainly not essential.

Here are some other ideas:
- Eggs boiled, poached or scrambled (see pages 125–6 for recipes).
- Grilled cheese, avocado, cooked ham, tomato, baked beans on toast, separately or in combinations. Cut into fingers.
- Ricotta cheese or yoghurt and fresh fruit. The fruit can be cut into pieces and served with the ricotta or yoghurt as a dip or mixed with mashed soft fruit and eaten with a spoon.

- Muffins are a good breakfast food (see pages 82–86 for recipes).
- Crumpets or bagels with suitable toppings.

Here are some extra breakfast recipes.

Emmanuel's Bread Dipped in Egg
• 1 TODDLER SERVE

1 egg, beaten
fingers of wholemeal bread
1 teaspoon butter
icing sugar and ground cinnamon, to serve

1. Dip the bread fingers in the beaten egg.
2. Heat the butter in a non-stick frying pan and gently cook the bread on both sides.
3. As a special treat, serve dusted with icing sugar and sprinkle with cinnamon.

Adam's Yoghurt and Fruit
• 2 TODDLER SERVES

My son, the good eater, would never eat cereal for breakfast but loved yoghurt and fruit, especially made up like this.

1 apple, peeled and grated
2 tablespoons orange juice
½ cup dried apricots or apples or a combination of both
½ cup rolled oats
3 tablespoons wheatgerm
1 tablespoon dark brown sugar
1 teaspoon grated lemon rind
200 g carton full-fat natural yoghurt or fruit-flavoured yoghurt if preferred

148

I. Mix the apple with the orange juice.

2. Combine with all the remaining ingredients and leave overnight in a covered container in the refrigerator.

3. Serve for breakfast.

Smoothies

Smoothies are healthy milkshakes whipped up in a blender. They can be a good way to get a breakfast substitute into a reluctant eater. They are also a good way to use up over-ripe fruit, especially bananas.

Smoothies should be consumed by toddlers from a cup, soon after being made. It's important not to put smoothies in bottles as the combination of milk and food being sucked from a teat over a period of time can cause black teeth and diarrhoea.

Sarah's Breakfast Smoothie
• 1 MOTHER AND TODDLER SERVE

2 small/1 large banana, peeled

2 cups full-fat milk

1 egg

1 teaspoon sugar, optional

5–6 drops vanilla flavouring essence

¼ teaspoon ground nutmeg

I. Mix all the ingredients in a blender or Bamix and serve.

2. Add a piece of toast, bread or rice cracker and you have a most satisfactory breakfast.

VARIATIONS

•   Try I cup of milk and I cup of natural yoghurt.

- Other fresh fruit can be used, such as pears, strawberries, peaches, nectarines or apricots.
- Use other sweeteners such as honey or maple syrup.
- For an extra breakfast boost, add a little wheatgerm or brewer's yeast.

CHAPTER 21

Main Courses

Couscous

Couscous is a wheat semolina, available in supermarkets. It is the traditional dish of North African countries and can be served both hot and cold with a variety of dishes.

To make couscous, pour 1 cup of boiling water into 1 cup of couscous. Stir, leave for a few minutes, then fluff up with a fork. Stock can be used instead of water for more flavour.

Spiced Couscous
LUNCH AS AN ACCOMPANIMENT
• FAMILY SERVE

2 cups couscous
2 teaspoons sultanas
1 clove
¼ teaspoon grated cinnamon
¼ teaspoon grated nutmeg
2 cups boiling water or stock
2 teaspoons butter

I. Put the couscous, sultanas, clove, cinnamon and nutmeg

into a bowl. Stir to mix through spices.

2. Pour on the boiling water or stock.

3. Allow to stand for 5 minutes, or until the water is absorbed.

4. Use a fork to stir through the butter.

5. Remove the clove. Serve hot.

Darcey's Couscous, Pasta or Rice
LUNCH OR DINNER
• EASY TODDLER MEAL

cooked couscous, pasta or rice
flaked canned tuna or finely chopped cooked meat or chicken
variety of steamed vegetables, diced
homemade tomato sauce (see pages 98–99) or commercial
    bottled Italian tomato sauce
grated cheese or natural yoghurt

Use the ingredients to make many different combinations depending on what's available; for example:
*   couscous, lamb, tomato sauce and yoghurt
*   pasta, tuna, tomato sauce and cheese
*   rice, ham, vegies, tomato sauce and cheese
    and so on
As your baby becomes a toddler, introduce things like pitted olives, capers and chopped, sun-dried tomatoes.

Fish

Fish Croquettes
LUNCH OR DINNER, FINGER FOOD
• 6–8 TODDLER SERVES • SUITABLE FOR FREEZING

2 potatoes
2 tablespoons grated onion and grated carrot
1 egg, beaten
180 g can tuna in springwater, drained and flaked
30 g Cheddar cheese, grated
2 tablespoons plain flour

1. Cook and mash the potatoes.
2. Stir the grated onion and carrot into the hot potatoes.
3. Combine the egg, tuna and cheese with the potato mixture.
4. Cool well, then shape into patties and roll in the flour.
5. Cook slowly in a lightly greased non-stick frying pan until golden on both sides, turning once.

Polenta

Polenta is cornmeal and is available in supermarkets or delicatessens. Polenta is a traditional northern Italian dish that can be eaten alone or as an accompaniment to many dishes. When it has cooled and hardened it can be sliced and fried, grilled or baked, and served with a variety of additional ingredients.

Polenta with Tomato Sauce
LUNCH, SNACK/FINGER FOOD
• FAMILY SERVE • 6–8 TODDLER SERVES

1 cup polenta
3 cups homemade stock (see pages 60–62) or water or half and half
2 tablespoons grated Parmesan cheese
1 tablespoon chopped fresh parsley
homemade tomato sauce to serve (see pages 98–99)

1. Grease and line a lamington tin.
2. Boil the stock and/or water in a heavy-based pan, then gradually add the polenta, stirring constantly.
3. Reduce the heat and cook for about 10 minutes, stirring constantly, until the polenta has the consistency of mashed potato.
4. Remove from the heat and stir in the cheese and parsley.
5. Spoon into the prepared tin. Cover and refrigerate until cold.
6. Cut the polenta into eight pieces and then grill (brushed with a little oil), or fry in about 2 tablespoons of oil or butter until golden. Top with hot tomato sauce.

Note: Cooked cold polenta makes great finger food.

Frittata

Frittata are Italian omelettes. A frittata is cooked slowly over a low heat. When cooked it is firm and set. It is flat and round and cooked on both sides.

You can use an endless variety of fillings such as cheese, herbs, vegetables and ham.

Frittata are easy, quick and popular and make great finger food.

Basic Frittata
LUNCH OR DINNER, SNACK/FINGER FOOD
• 4 TODDLER SERVES

1 tablespoon olive oil
300 g small zucchini (about 3 zucchini), thinly sliced
4 eggs, lightly beaten
100 ml full-cream milk
pepper

1. Heat the oil in a heavy-based frying pan and sauté the zucchini over a low heat for about 10–15 minutes, or until soft.
2. Mix the eggs, milk and pepper together and pour over the zucchini.
3. Cook until set underneath. Turn it over or put the pan under a medium to hot grill for a few minutes, or until the frittata is golden and set.

VARIATIONS
- Add sliced onions, leeks, mushrooms, tomatoes, capsicum or other leftover vegetables and cook with the zucchini.
- Add grated Cheddar or Parmesan cheese to the egg mixture, or sprinkle over before grilling the frittata.

Chicken

Chicken Pasta Bake
LUNCH OR DINNER
• FAMILY SERVE

250 g (2 cups) cooked fusilli pasta
125 g cottage cheese
3 eggs
1 tablespoon vegetable oil
1 onion, finely chopped
500 g minced lean chicken
400 g can tomatoes, chopped
½ cup water
2 tablespoons homemade tomato sauce (see pages 98–99) or
    commercial Italian tomato sauce
300 ml carton fresh cream or ½ cream and ½ natural yoghurt
1½ cups grated Cheddar cheese
fresh breadcrumbs

1. Preheat the oven to 180°C. In a mixing bowl, mix the pasta, cottage cheese and 1 egg. Put into a greased baking dish.

2. In a frying pan, heat the oil and sauté the onion until soft.

3. Add the chicken and cook until it changes colour, stirring frequently.

4. Add the tomatoes, water and tomato sauce. Simmer until the sauce thickens, about 20 minutes, and then pour over the pasta mixture.

5. Beat the remaining eggs with the cream. Mix in the cheese and spoon over the chicken mixture. Sprinkle with breadcrumbs.

6. Bake for 30 minutes.

7. Puree or mouli portions for your baby.

Jann's Pate
LUNCH, PARTY FOOD, SNACK/FINGER FOOD
• FAMILY SERVE

125 g butter
2 rindless rashers of bacon, chopped
1 large onion, peeled and finely chopped
1 clove garlic, finely sliced
grated nutmeg
ground black pepper
500 g chicken livers, trimmed and chopped
1 teaspoon salt
1 tablespoon chopped fresh coriander or parsley
1 tablespoon brandy

1. Put the butter, bacon, onion, garlic, nutmeg and pepper in a large, heavy-based frying pan. Cook over a medium heat for 5 minutes, stirring frequently.

2. Add the livers and salt. Cook, stirring frequently, for about 5–10 minutes, until all the livers change colour.

3. Stir in the coriander and brandy. Cool slightly.

4. Mix in a food processor to a smooth texture, then put into several small bowls or one large bowl and refrigerate until set.

5. Serve spread on fingers of toast or rusks.

Spicy Chicken Wings
LUNCH OR DINNER, PARTY FOOD, SNACK/FINGER FOOD
• 3–4 TODDLERS OR FAMILY SERVE

4 tablespoons salt-reduced soy sauce
1 tablespoon sesame oil
1 tablespoon honey
1 clove garlic, crushed
1 teaspoon grated ginger root
1 tablespoon teriyaki marinade
1 tablespoon water
12 chicken wings

1. Combine all the ingredients, apart from the chicken wings, in a shallow china or glass ovenproof dish.
2. Add the chicken wings; turn over to coat and marinate in the mixture for 3 hours.
3. Preheat the oven to 180°C.
4. Bake the chicken for 30–40 minutes, turning once, or until cooked through.

Potatoes and Rice

Zintgraff Swiss Jacket Potatoes
LUNCH OR DINNER
• FAMILY SERVE OR 1 POTATO/1 TODDLER MEAL

4 medium potatoes
4 tablespoons ricotta cheese
4 tablespoons mashed avocado
2 tablespoons grated Gruyère or Jarlsburg cheese

1. Preheat the oven to 220°C.

2. Wash and prick the potatoes. Bake on the shelf for 30 minutes, or until cooked.

3. Cut the cooked potatoes in half lengthways. Scoop out the centre and mash well. Add the avocado and ricotta to the mashed potato and stir to mix.

4. Refill the potato cases with the mixture.

5. Sprinkle with grated cheese.

6. Heat in the oven for 10 minutes or until the cheese is golden and bubbling hot.

VARIATIONS

- Endless combinations are possible, such as baked beans, left-over cooked lentils, canned tuna or chopped cooked ham.

Savoury Rice Loaf
LUNCH OR DINNER
• FAMILY SERVE

2 cups cooked long-grain rice
1 cup finely shredded spinach
2 cups ricotta or cottage cheese
½ cup homemade tomato sauce (see pages 98–99)
310 g can sweetcorn kernels, drained
1 egg, beaten

I. Preheat the oven to 180°C.

2. Combine all the ingredients in a bowl and mix thoroughly.

3. Spoon into a greased loaf tin.

4. Bake for 45 minutes or until set.

Meat

Once your toddler can eat harder-to-chew food such as meat and chicken, she can eat meat, chicken or fish, accompanied by steamed vegetables, pasta, rice or salad. Both my kids (even the fussy eater) always enjoyed crumbed veal fillet or flattened crumbed chicken breast.

Crumbed Veal Fillet
DINNER
• FAMILY SERVE • GOOD FINGER FOOD CUT INTO STRIPS

4 thin fillets of veal (if necessary flatten with a mallet or rolling pin), cut into finger-long strips
1 cup plain flour
1 egg, beaten
1 cup dry breadcrumbs
½ cup vegetable oil

1. Coat the veal in the flour, the egg and the breadcrumbs, in this order.
2. Heat the oil in a frying pan until hot.
3. Cook the veal quickly in sizzling oil, on both sides, until crisp and brown.
4. Remove immediately and drain on kitchen paper towels.
5. Serve with lightly steamed vegetables or salad.

VARIATION
• Flatten 2 skinless chicken breast fillets with a meat mallet or rolling pin. Cut each breast into strips, coat and cook as above. Chicken may need a little longer cooking time than the veal.

It's always a good idea to do any sort of cooking involving frying or the use of large amounts of hot oil when babies and toddlers are not underfoot.

Kate's Little Meatballs
LUNCH OR DINNER, SNACK/FINGER FOOD
• 6–8 TODDLER SERVES • SUITABLE FOR FREEZING

One of the few foods my daughter would eat.

500 g finely minced veal
1 onion, peeled and grated
1 tablespoon oyster sauce
1 tablespoon salt-reduced soy sauce
1 egg, beaten
vegetable oil, for cooking

1. Combine all the ingredients in a bowl and mix thoroughly.
2. Roll into little balls in clean, cold hands.
3. Cook in a frying pan in a little heated oil over medium heat until they have turned brown and are cooked through.
4. Drain on kitchen paper towels before serving.

VARIATION
• Finely minced lean chicken, lamb or beef may be used.

Meatloaf in a Hurry
LUNCH OR DINNER
• FAMILY SERVE • SUITABLE FOR FREEZING

This dish can be thrown together in 30 minutes and, combined with brown rice, steamed carrots and broccoli, it is a good balance of healthy food for all the family.

500 g finely minced lean beef
1 onion, peeled and finely chopped
1 carrot, chopped
1 egg, beaten
1 teaspoon Vegemite
1 tablespoon tomato sauce
1 tablespoon fruit chutney
ground black pepper

1. Preheat the oven to 180°C.
2. Combine all the ingredients in a bowl and mix thoroughly.
3. Spoon the mixture into a 1 kg loaf tin lined with grease-proof paper or baking powder.
4. Bake for 1 hour or until cooked.
5. To microwave, cook in a microwave-safe dish on medium setting, for 20 minutes. Serve hot.

The Barker Tacos
DINNER, FINGER FOOD
• FAMILY SERVE

Tacos are Mexican corn pancakes shaped into shells that you fill with a variety of foods. We first discovered tacos in the seventies when we were living in North America and they quickly became part of the weekly menu. Toddlers like the taste of the shells and enjoy filling them up from the dishes on the table and the general mess generated. Yes, my fussy eater would eat tacos (only, of course, with very select items of food for the filling – nothing green).

250 g finely minced lean beef
2 tablespoons fresh chopped parsley
1 teaspoon paprika
1 square dark chocolate, grated
2 tablespoons homemade beef stock (see pages 61–62) or water
1 cup tomato puree
½ red capsicum, seeded and finely chopped
1 large mushroom, finely chopped
1 carrot, peeled and grated
1 zucchini, finely chopped
1 cup water
1 cup canned red kidney beans
taco shells (available from supermarkets)

1. Cook the minced beef in a heavy-based pan over medium to high heat with the parsley, paprika, chocolate and stock until finely crumbed and brown, stirring frequently.
2. Add the tomato puree and stir well.
3. Add all the vegetables (except the red kidney beans), water and simmer, covered, for 1 hour.
4. Add the beans and simmer for 30 minutes.
5. Place the meat mixture in a warm serving dish.

The meat mixture goes into the base of the taco shell. Other ingredients are piled on top. It's all a bit messy but yummy. Have plenty of paper napkins to hand.

SUGGESTIONS FOR FILLINGS
Serve in dishes placed on the table:
Shredded crisp lettuce
Sliced tomato
Diced red onion
Grated cheese
Grated carrot
Sliced beetroot
Sliced cucumber
Pitted olives
Sliced avocado

Pizzas

Small, instant pizza bases can be made from crumpets, Turkish or any flat bread, English muffins, Lebanese bread (pita bread) or thick slices of bread. Pizza bases are also available ready-made in supermarkets.

Basic tomato sauce (see pages 98–99) can be used to spread on the base before adding other toppings.

It you would like to make your own base here's a simple scone method. Mini pizzas work well for toddlers who like to 'have their own'.

Wholemeal Pizza Base (scone base)
LUNCH OR DINNER, PARTY FOOD, SNACK/FINGER FOOD
• MAKES APPROXIMATELY 2 DINNER-PLATE SIZE BASES • SUITABLE FOR FREEZING

30 g butter
2 cups self-raising wholemeal flour
½ cup milk
½ cup water

1. Preheat the oven to 200°C.

2. Rub the butter into the flour in a mixing bowl until it resembles coarse breadcrumbs.

3. Make a well in the centre. Pour in the combined milk and water. Stir with a round-bladed knife to form a stiff dough.

4. Knead very lightly on a floured board. Divide in half. Roll or pat each half into a round shape I cm thick and place on two oiled baking trays.

5. Cover with the topping mix and bake for 20–30 minutes.

Topping Ideas

Tomato and Cheese

homemade tomato sauce (see pages 98–99)
2 tomatoes, thinly sliced
½ green capsicum, thinly sliced
1 small onion, peeled and finely chopped
6 mushrooms, sliced
1 cup grated Tasty cheese
1 cup grated Mozzarella cheese
1 tablespoon chopped fresh basil

1. Preheat the oven to 200°C.

2. Spread the chosen base with the tomato sauce.

3. Top evenly with the tomatoes, capsicum, onion and mushrooms.

4. Sprinkle with the cheese and bake for 20–30 minutes.

Tuna, Capsicum and Sweetcorn

homemade tomato sauce (see pages 98–99)
180 g can tuna, drained
1 green capsicum, seeded and finely chopped
½ cup sweetcorn kernels
1 cup grated Mozzarella cheese

1. Preheat the oven to 200°C.
2. Spread the chosen base with the tomato sauce.
3. Scatter the tuna over the sauce. Arrange the capsicum and the sweetcorn kernels over the tuna.
5. Cover with the cheese and bake for 20–30 minutes.

OTHER TOPPING INGREDIENTS (USE IN ANY COMBINATION)
Sliced sautéed onions, lightly cooked button mushrooms, zucchini, broccoli, a variety of cheeses, (ricotta, Jarlsburg, Gruyère, or Edam), salami, peperoni, ham, bacon, pineapple chunks, chopped fresh herbs such as basil, sage or oregano, fresh sliced tomato.

Stir-fry

Stir-frying is a simple, quick and healthy way to cook. Non-vegie-eating toddlers will often eat stir-fried vegetables. The food is tossed in a small amount of very hot oil which seals the surfaces, retaining moisture and flavour.

Stir-fried food is easy to pick up with the fingers, which makes it good food for toddlers to share with the family.

Here are a few stir-fry tips:
• Have all the ingredients ready before you start. Cut meat or poultry across the grain into slivers or small pieces. Cut vegetables evenly into matchsticks or thin slices.

- Heat the pan or wok over a high heat for 1–2 minutes before adding the oil.
- To prevent burning, keep the food moving at all times, but don't move meat until it starts to brown.
- Eat stir-fries as soon as they are cooked.

Noodle and Vegetable Stir-fry
LUNCH OR DINNER, FINGER FOOD
• FAMILY SERVE

2 tablespoons peanut oil
1 small zucchini, sliced
1 stalk celery, chopped
1 carrot, chopped
½ cup broccoli florets
½ cup sliced green beans
½ cup cauliflower florets
½ red or green capsicum, seeded and chopped
500 g Hokkien noodles
1 teaspoon brown sugar
2 teaspoons salt-reduced soy sauce

1. Heat the oil in a wok or large frying pan.
2. Stir-fry the zucchini, celery, carrot, broccoli, beans, cauliflower and capsicum for 2–3 minutes.
3. Add the noodles and sprinkle with sugar.
4. Add the soy sauce and stir-fry constantly.
5. Add 1 tablespoon water and stir-fry for a further 2–3 minutes, then serve.

Pork and Cabbage Stir-fry
LUNCH OR DINNER, FINGER FOOD
• FAMILY SERVE

½ Chinese cabbage, finely shredded and tough stalks removed
1 bunch spinach, washed and shredded
2 tablespoons peanut oil
375 g pork fillet, sliced
2 cloves garlic, finely chopped
2 tablespoons crunchy peanut butter
juice of 1 lemon

1. Put the cabbage and spinach into a saucepan with a small amount of water.
2. Cook for 3–5 minutes, stirring once to move around. Drain well.
3. Heat the oil in a wok or frying pan and fry the pork until golden.
4. Add the garlic and stir through the pork.
5. Add the peanut butter and lemon juice and stir-fry for 1 minute.
6. Add the spinach and cabbage and stir-fry until heated through.
7. Serve with rice or noodles.

Stir-fried Liver with Vegetables
LUNCH OR DINNER, FINGER FOOD
• FAMILY SERVE

2 tablespoons peanut oil
1 teaspoon grated ginger root
1 red onion, sliced
1 red capsicum, seeded and sliced

375 g lamb's liver, sliced
1 cup fresh bean sprouts
1 tablespoon salt-reduced soy sauce
1 tablespoon sesame seeds

1. Heat the oil in a wok and stir-fry the ginger, onion and capsicum until the onion is soft.
2. Add the liver and stir-fry for 3 minutes, until no longer pink – don't overdo it.
3. Add the bean sprouts and soy sauce and stir-fry for I minute.
4. Sprinkle with sesame seeds. Serve with rice or noodles.

Stir-fried Chicken and Rice
DINNER, FINGER FOOD
• FAMILY SERVE

1 cup brown rice
3 cups homemade chicken stock (see page 60)
2 tablespoons peanut oil
4 skinless chicken breast fillets, thinly sliced
1 onion, peeled and chopped
1 stick celery, thinly sliced
½ red capsicum, seeded and cut into strips
1½ cups frozen peas
1 tablespoon salt-reduced soy sauce
3 eggs, beaten

1. Cook the rice in the chicken stock according to the instructions on the packet. Set aside.
2. Heat the oil in a wok and stir-fry the chicken until it starts to change colour. Add the onion, celery and capsicum to the wok and continue cooking until the chicken is golden.

3. Add rice, peas and soy sauce. Stir-fry for 3 minutes. Set aside.

4. Cook the eggs gently until firm in a non-stick frying pan. Cut into squares with a spatula.

5. Toss onto the stir-fry and serve immediately.

VARIATIONS
- Substitute beef rump steak for chicken.
- Use other vegetables such as canned bamboo shoots, canned baby corn and mushrooms.

Tofu Stir-fry
LUNCH OR DINNER
• FAMILY SERVE

500 g tofu
2 tablespoons salt-reduced soy sauce
juice of 1 lime
2 tablespoons vegetable oil
2 large onions, peeled and thinly sliced
1 capsicum, seeded and sliced
1 tablespoon finely chopped ginger
1 teaspoon sugar

1. Cut the tofu into cubes and pat dry. Place in a shallow bowl and sprinkle with soy sauce and lime juice. Set aside.

2. Heat the oil in a wok or a large frying pan and stir-fry the onions, capsicum and ginger for 3 minutes.

3. Add the tofu and marinade to the wok and sprinkle with the sugar.

4. Continue stir-frying for 1–2 minutes, or until hot. Serve with rice.

Salads

Salads are nutritious and healthy and make great finger food, but care has to be taken that there are no little hard 'bits' which can be a choking hazard. Whole raw apple, carrot, nuts (unless ground) and chunks of raw celery are potential problems and it is now recommend not to give these to children until the age of 4.

Base your toddler's first salads around familiar foods, then gradually introduce her to new ingredients. Babies can start to eat things like tomato, cucumber, grated carrot and apple, beetroot (if you can stand the mess) from 6–9 months of age. Anytime between 9–15 months they can eat most types of salad.

Always start with small amounts. If it gets eaten, add more to the plate.

DRESSINGS

Use a light dressing or orange, lemon, apple juice or natural yoghurt in the first year. After 1 year, a little of any of the traditional dressings can be used, including mayonnaise.

Basic Salad
LUNCH OR DINNER, FINGER FOOD
• 1–2 TODDLER SERVES, DEPENDING ON AMOUNTS USED

1 very small crisp lettuce leaf
grated carrot
grated cheese
2–3 cherry tomatoes, halved
1 slice cucumber
1–2 orange segments

I. Top the lettuce with the carrot, cheese, tomatoes and cucumber and arrange the orange segments around the salad.

VARIATION

- Add diced cooked ham or chicken or ricotta cheese instead of grated cheese.

Ricotta and Date Salad
LUNCH OR DINNER, FINGER FOOD
• 1 TODDLER SERVE

1 small crisp lettuce leaf
½ cup ricotta cheese
2 teaspoons red capsicum, seeded and finely chopped
1 tablespoon chopped fresh dates, seeded

1. Place the lettuce leaf in a serving bowl.
2. Combine all the other ingredients together and spoon onto the lettuce leaf.

Potato Salad
LUNCH OR DINNER, FINGER FOOD
• 1–2 TODDLER SERVES

1 potato, cooked and diced
½ tablespoon mayonnaise
½ tablespoon low-fat yoghurt
1 teaspoon chopped fresh parsley
1 tablespoon diced cooked lean ham

1. Toss the potato with the other ingredients.

Pineapple and Ham Salad
LUNCH OR DINNER, FINGER FOOD
• 1–2 TODDLER SERVES

½ cup crushed canned pineapple
1 cup diced cooked lean ham
1 tablespoon shredded bean sprouts
1 tablespoon red capsicum, seeded and finely chopped

1. Combine all the ingredients.
2. Toss with a little of the juice from the crushed pineapple.

Sarah and Miriam's Tuna Salad
LUNCH OR DINNER
FAMILY SERVE

185 g can tuna
1 tomato, chopped
1 small Lebanese cucumber, chopped
1 tablespoon shredded mint

DRESSING
½ cup plain yoghurt
1 teaspoon wholegrain mustard

1. Mix all the salad ingredients together gently.
2. Combine the yoghurt and mustard and stir though the tuna salad.

CHAPTER 22

Sandwiches

Sandwiches are the fundamental quick food and, once babies can handle finger food, are ideal for lunch or dinner. Most babies can start to eat sandwiches by 12 months if not before. Avoid bread with seeds until well into the second year. Leave the crusts on – even if they get chewed and sucked on then spat out they provide good exercise for jaws and help your baby get used to firmer food. Remember, if your baby or toddler eats like a bird, make bird-size sandwiches!

Use a variety of breads such as lavash, pita, rolls, bagels, white, wholemeal and so on.

Some Sandwich Ideas

EASY BASICS

Vegemite, peanut butter (over 12 months), ricotta or cottage cheese, cream cheese, grated Cheddar, tomato, cucumber, banana, avocado, pate, grated carrot, lean beef, lamb or pork, meatloaf, chicken, canned tuna or canned salmon, egg.

SPREAD SUGGESTIONS

- Mayonnaise
- Chicken Puree
- Jann's Pate
- Hoummos
- Mashed avocado

COMBINATION IDEAS

- Grated cheese and carrot with a little mayonnaise
- Peanut butter and mashed banana
- Grated cheese and Vegemite
- Cold scrambled eggs with thinly sliced frankfurts
- Mashed dried dates and cream cheese (seed the dates and cook in a little water to soften them), or use fresh dates
- Avocado with just about anything
- Salmon and grated cucumber
- Ham and avocado
- Grated apple, cheese and mayonnaise
- Canned tuna and yoghurt
- Peanut butter and jam (or jelly as it is known in North America – my daughter lived on peanut butter and jelly sandwiches for many years)
- Canned creamed corn, ricotta cheese and a little shredded lettuce
- Cream cheese, sliced banana and a sprinkle of ground cinnamon

Novelty Sandwiches for Fussy Eaters

Good luck with these ideas. They are suitable for older toddlers. You know your own tolerance level for messy games with food. As long as it's being eaten, fine, but if it turns into a non-eating play event call a halt.

HEALTHY FACES

On individual plates make a face on the bread:
- Grated carrot or yellow cheese for hair
- Lebanese cucumber strips for nose and eyebrows
- Red capsicum for lips
- Cherry tomato halves for eyes and earrings
- Sultanas for a necklace
- Blobs of hommus for cheeks

A range of shapes such as caterpillars, animals, cars and houses can be made with a little imagination using a variety of foods if you are so inclined and if you think it will encourage your toddler to eat.

TIGER TOAST

Toasted wholemeal bread spread with strips of Vegemite and margarine or butter.

SANDWICH SHAPES (FOR OLDER TODDLERS)

Let your toddler make their own shapes out of the bread with large biscuit cutters, hearts, stars and so on.

Put a small amount of suitable sandwich fillings on plates and let them make their own combinations of the shapes.

Pinwheel Sandwiches

3 slices of bread with the crusts cut off
2 or 3 different sandwich fillings such as:
- smooth peanut butter (over 12 months)
- honey (over 12 months)
- chopped dates
- Vegemite
- grated cheese
- thinly sliced cold roast meat (eg chicken)
- sliced tomato
- sliced sweet pickled gherkins or gherkin spread

1. Spread the fillings onto one side of the different slices of bread.
2. Place each on top of the other. Roll tightly.
3. Cut across the roll into slices so each looks like a pinwheel.

CHAPTER 23

Fast Food

There are lots of recipes throughout the book that can be assembled very quickly. For example:
* Eggs boiled, poached or scrambled
* Thin Chinese Omelette
* Sylvia's Tomato and Poached Egg
* Couscous
* Noodle and Vegetable Stir-fry
* Most of the salad recipes
* Sandwiches
* Bread Dipped in Egg

Other quick ideas:
* Fish fingers and salad
* Canned baked beans or canned spaghetti on toast
* Grilled cooked ham, cheese and tomato on toast, or in jaffles
* Soup
* Fruit salad with yoghurt
* Leftovers

Snack Food for Toddlers

Snacking tips

Many toddlers seem to need small snacks throughout the day. As long as the snacks are nutritious, this is quite okay.

However, if your toddler does snack a lot, chances are she will not eat much at mealtimes. Once again, as long as the snacks are of good quality this doesn't matter, but if you are concerned try to give only a small snack at morning and afternoon tea time and resist the whinges at other times.

Snacks to avoid

Bearing in mind that occasional indulgences are okay, avoid the following snack foods as much as possible. A constant intake of these sorts of food not only lays the foundation for possible problems later, but also does not give toddlers the best chance for optimum development.

- Top of the list is unlimited amounts of liquid in bottles or from cups with teats. Toddlers are often never really hungry because of their milk, juice and water consumption. If your toddler still has bottles, try to cut down to two bottles of milk a day (morning and night) and use a cup during the day. Try to avoid giving drinks an hour before meals and offer liquid after the food, not before.
- Sweet or salty biscuits
- Packs containing fatty and salty snacks
- Commercial fruit sticks
- Lollies
- Chips or crisps
- Iceblocks
- Snack bars
- Chocolates

- Syrups, cordial
- Chocolate spreads, jam and honey (a little jam and honey is fine from time to time)

Try these snacks instead:
- Pikelets
- Instant pizza
- A small sandwich
- Polenta
- Smoothies
- Muffins
- Frittata
- Crumpets, bagels or English muffins
- Fresh fruit
- Frozen fruit
- Fruit salad
- Grissini sticks
- Cruskets
- Yoghurt as it comes, or frozen
- Fromage frais
- Raisin loaf
- Cereal, plain or with milk
- Wedges of hard-boiled egg
- Wedges of tomato
- Cheese sticks
- Cheese slices
- Quick-cooking noodles, plain or with cheese
- Iceblocks made from fruit juice
- Dried fruit

CHAPTER 24

Desserts

Desserts are not essential and can be very simple ideas such as fresh fruit and yoghurt.

The following recipes are for times when you feel like having dessert.

Grandma Dot's Spanish Cream
• FAMILY SERVE

2 eggs, separated
2 tablespoons sugar
2 cups milk
10 g sachet gelatine
⅓ cup hot water
a few drops of vanilla flavouring essence

1. Beat the egg yolks and sugar together. Add the milk and beat well.
2. Heat in a saucepan, stirring with a wooden spoon until the mixture is of thin custard consistency.
3. Dissolve the gelatine in the hot water, then add to the mixture.

4. Stir well over low heat. Do not allow to boil.

5. Set aside to cool.

6. Beat the egg whites until soft peaks form and fold into the mixture.

7. Flavour with vanilla.

8. Pour into individual moulds or a large mould and chill until set.

Traditional Stirred Egg Custard
• FAMILY SERVE

1 cup milk
1 egg
1 tablespoon sugar
½ teaspoon vanilla flavouring essence

1. Warm the milk in the top of a double boiler over gently boiling water.

2. Whisk the egg, sugar and vanilla together.

3. Add to the warm milk.

4. Stir with a wooden spoon until the custard coats the spoon (takes about 10–20 minutes).

5. Do not allow to overheat or the custard will curdle.

6. When ready, pour into a jug and cover the top of the custard with clear plastic wrap – this stops a skin from forming on the custard.

Fay's Steamed Cup Custard
• 4 TODDLER SERVES

1 egg, lightly beaten
½ cup milk
sugar and vanilla flavouring essence to taste

1. Mix the egg, milk, sugar and vanilla together with a fork.
2. Place in a mug or cup.
3. Stand in a small saucepan with water halfway up the cup. Bring to the boil and cook for approximately 3 minutes.
4. Remove from the heat and allow to stand and cool.

Chocolate Pudding with Mashed Pear
• **1–2 TODDLER SERVES**

½ cup milk
1 teaspoon sugar
1 teaspoon drinking chocolate powder
1 egg, lightly beaten
½ very ripe pear, cored, peeled and mashed

1. Warm the milk in the top of a double boiler over simmering water.
2. Add the sugar and drinking chocolate powder.
3. Reduce the heat and stir in the beaten egg.
4. Keep stirring over a gentle heat until the custard thickens (takes about 10–20 minutes).
5. Pour over the mashed pear.

Grandma Dot's Bread Pudding
• **FAMILY SERVE**

4 eggs
2 teaspoons sugar
2 cups milk
a few drops vanilla flavouring essence
1½ cups fresh breadcrumbs
½ cup sultanas

1. Preheat the oven to 150°C.

2. Beat the eggs and sugar together. Add the milk and vanilla.
3. Place the breadcrumbs and sultanas into a lightly greased baking dish.
4. Pour the custard mixture over this and stir gently.
5. Bake for ½–I hour, or until custard is set.

VARIATION
• To make a meringue topping, reserve two egg whites when beating the eggs and sugar. When the custard is partly set, whisk the egg whites until stiff peaks form. Whisk in ½ cup caster sugar until soft and spread on top of the pudding. Return to oven for 30 minutes.

Junket from Mavis
• 4 TODDLER SERVES

1 cup lukewarm milk
½ junket tablet, dissolved in 1 teaspoon water
½ teaspoon sugar
a few drops vanilla flavouring essence

I. Gradually pour the warm milk onto the dissolved junket tablet, stirring as you do so.
2. Pour the mixture into small moulds. (One large mould causes the mixture to separate once the surface has been cut.)
3. Allow to set, then refrigerate.
4. Delicious served with stewed fruit.

Kate's Favourite Fruit Salad
• FAMILY SERVE

1 cup cubed watermelon
1 cup cubed rockmelon
1 punnet strawberries, sliced
1 punnet blueberries
1 cup cubed mango
yoghurt

I. Combine the prepared fruit in a bowl.
2. Serve with yoghurt.

Narelle's Apricot Mousse
• FAMILY SERVE

500 g dried apricots
sugar to taste
½ teaspoon vanilla flavouring essence
200 g natural yoghurt

I. Simmer the apricots, in water to cover, for 25 minutes.
2. Stir in the sugar, if used, and cook a further 5 minutes.
3. Stir in the vanilla, then the yoghurt.
4. Put into small pots and chill thoroughly.

PART FIVE

TREATS AND CELEBRATIONS

CHAPTER 25

Birthday Parties

Birthday parties can be lots of fun or absolute nightmares. By the time your children are 21 you will find you have had your share of both. Roger and I often reminisce about various parties and it's the disastrous ones that make us laugh the most now. Generally the most successful ones were out of doors and tied in to some activity (water slides, national parks).

Disasters for us tended to be the ones we tried the hardest at and were invariably held indoors with lots of children and organised 'games'.

Notable failures include the time when we scraped together enough money to hire a clown who none of the children liked – I spent the afternoon counselling the clown. At my daughter's third birthday I provided a particular sort of noisy banger thing that frightened the life out of all the children, who started sobbing hysterically just as their parents arrived to pick them up.

I have included in this book many recipes that can be used, and many are suitable for picnics. May your birthday parties be memorable.

Look in the index for any of the following:
• Muffins

- Polenta with Tomato Sauce
- Basic Frittata
- Jann's Pate
- Kate's Little Meatballs
- Spicy Chicken Wings
- Pizza
- Sandwiches
- Pikelets
- Frog in a Pond
- Jann's Avocado Dip
- And for the birthday cake . . . Grandma Elly's Swiss Gugelhupf

Frog in a Pond

1 packet green jelly
6 chocolate frogs

1. Prepare the jelly.
2. Divide among 6 little bowls (or more if the jelly allows).
3. When the jelly is almost set, plop a chocolate frog in the centre.

Pikelets

1 cup self-raising flour
a pinch of salt
½ teaspoon sodium bicarbonate
2 tablespoons sugar
1 large egg
2 teaspoons melted butter
⅔ cup of milk

1. Mix all the ingredients and beat until the batter is thick and smooth.

2. Let stand for 2 hours before use.

3. Heat a frying pan and lightly grease the base.

4. Put spoonfuls of batter into the pan and cook until bubbles form on the surface. Flip over and cook the other side.

5. Wrap cooked pikelets in a tea towel to keep warm.

6. Eat with butter, cream, jam or honey, or all four.

Grandma Elly's Swiss Guglhupf

This is the family Zintgraff's traditional birthday cake – loved by children as well as adults. It looks great and tastes greater – there's never a crumb left.

185 g unsalted butter
1 cup caster sugar
4 x 50 g eggs, beaten
½ cup milk
1 teaspoon vanilla flavouring essence
2 cups plain flour, sifted
3 teaspoons baking powder
1 teaspoon salt
450 g dark cooking chocolate, grated

1. Preheat the oven to 170°C.

2. Cream the butter and sugar together in a mixing bowl with an electric mixer until light and fluffy.

3. Gradually add the eggs and beat well after each addition.

4. Add the milk and vanilla alternately with the dry ingredients and stir gently until evenly combined.

5. Spoon half the mixture into a well-greased guglhupf tin.

6. Sprinkle with the grated chocolate.

7. Spread the rest of the cake mixture evenly over the chocolate.

8. Bake for 1 hour or until a warm skewer inserted in the centre comes out clear.

9. Remove from the oven and allow to stand for 15 minutes in the tin before turning out onto a wire cooling rack to cool completely.

10. Dust with icing sugar and serve.

Play Dough

What is life with toddlers without a little play dough to mess about with? Apart from the fun of playing, toddlers enjoy helping make it. Here's a recipe:

2 cups plain flour
1 cup salt
2 tablespoons oil
a little water
food colouring

1. Mix the flour and salt together in a mixing bowl. Add the oil and a little water and knead to form a soft dough.

2. Too watery? Add more flour.

3. Too dry? Add more water.

4. Store in an airtight container or a plastic bag.

Finger Paint

And while we're on the subject of messing around, how about a little finger painting? Here's a recipe for finger paint:

½ cup cornflour
2 tablespoons white sugar
2 cups cold water
food colouring

1. Combine all the ingredients in a saucepan.
2. Stir constantly over a low to medium heat until the mixture boils and thickens, then allow to cool.
3. Pour into little containers and add a variety of edible food colouring.

Have fun . . .

CHAPTER 26

Celebrating Sydney's Annual City to Surf

The City to Surf is an annual run held in August. The course is 14 kilometres and runs from the city to Bondi Beach. It takes in some of the most exciting and lovely parts of Sydney. Forty thousand people now take part, from top runners to families and friends walking and pushing strollers. Crowds line the streets, bands play on rooftops, and it has become a day of celebration and thanksgiving for our wonderful city. And our fabulous climate — it has never rained on a City to Surf day.

Our family has participated in the City to Surf for many years and it is a tradition to have a lunch at our place after the event. It's a great time of year to eat outdoors as although it's winter, the crisp sunny August days are ideal for picnics. Everyone brings a plate and the crowd always includes a few babies and toddlers who share the food. Even the fussy eaters eat well on City to Surf day.

Jann's Avocado Dip

Jann makes two bowls of this, which everyone attacks the minute they arrive after the run. The children love it and it is usually finished before the rest of the food is assembled.

2 avocados, mashed
juice of 1 lime or ½ lemon
3 spring onions, finely chopped
2 tablespoons cream (or olive oil – I like cream best)
2 tablespoons chopped coriander
½ teaspoon chilli sauce or a few drops of tabasco

1. Combine all the ingredients. Sprinkle a little of the lime or lemon juice over the top and leave the avocado stone in the middle of the dip to prevent the avocado going brown.
2. Serve with corn chips or on bread or cracker biscuits for children under 4.

Rob's Corned Meat
• SERVES 8–10

1½–2 kg (½ lb) corned topside (in a 'chunk')
water
1 tablespoon balsamic vinegar
1 tablespoon brown sugar
2 fresh bay leaves
2 large cloves garlic, crushed
freshly ground pepper

1. Place corned meat in a large pot and cover with water.
2. Add the vinegar, brown sugar, bay leaves, garlic and freshly ground pepper. Give the water a good swirl to mix all the ingredients.
3. Leave meat to soak for 24 hours – in winter it doesn't need to go in the fridge.

TO COOK MEAT

Bring water to the boil and quickly reduce to a very gentle simmer. Simmer meat for 1 hour. Leave in the water until ready to serve. After serving, put the meat back in the water and leave until the water is cold.

Rob's Ratatouille
• SERVES 6–8

I have been making this for years and have developed it into a bit of an art form. It is different from the way ratatouille is often made, which is as a stew.

In this recipe everything is cooked separately, then put together and heated through in the oven, hopefully without boiling.

It is time-consuming and uses quantities of very hot oil, so is best done without children underfoot when you have a few hours to spare (joke). However, it is absolutely delicious either hot or at room temperature and is a great vegetarian dish. It is best made a day or two before being eaten as the flavour improves with age! It will last in the fridge in a clean container for up to a week.

8 large zucchini
2 medium eggplant
sprinkle of salt
1 large red capsicum
1 large red onion
2 large cloves garlic, crushed
10–12 cooking tomatoes
3 tablespoons chopped fresh basil
3 tablespoons chopped fresh parsley

freshly ground pepper
a good quantity of a combination of light olive oil and canola oil
for deep frying
roll of absorbent kitchen paper

1. Wash the zucchini and eggplant.
2. Cut into thick strips and place in 2 large bowls.
3. Sprinkle with a little salt, toss and leave for 1 hour.

TO MAKE THE TOMATO SAUCE

1. Deseed and slice the capsicum. Peel and slice the onion. Peel, core and roughly chop the tomatoes.
2. Heat 1 tablespoon of olive oil in a heavy-based frypan.
3. Stir-fry the capsicum, onion and garlic for 5–10 minutes over high heat.
4. Add the tomatoes, half the basil and the pepper and continue stirring for a few minutes.
5. Turn down the heat and gently simmer the mixture with a lid on for 1 hour. After 1 hour remove the lid and simmer for another 20 minutes or so.
6. Add the remainder of the basil at the end of the cooking.

TO PREPARE AND COOK THE EGGPLANT AND ZUCCHINI

1. Wipe the moisture off the strips of eggplant and zucchini.
2. Heat enough oil (I use half light olive oil and half canola) in a heavy-based frying pan to quickly deep-fry the eggplant and zucchini. The oil should be hot and sizzling. You can speed things up by using two or even three frying pans.
3. As each batch comes off the stove place the vegie strips on absorbent kitchen paper.

TO ASSEMBLE THE RATATOUILLE

1. Line a baking dish with strips of eggplant and zucchini.

2. Cover with a layer of the tomato sauce.

3. Sprinkle with parsley.

4. Repeat the layers until the dish is full, ending with a layer of vegetables.

5. Place in a slow oven (150°C) for 30 minutes. Do not allow to boil.

Alain's Lentil Salad

Once again, this recipe comes from the Zintgraff kitchen. Nutritious, easy to make and yummy – I could eat this by the bowlful.

> 2 cups small greeny/brown lentils (or any other small lentils available), soaked for 2 hours
> 250 g bacon or ham (optional for vegetarians)
> 1 large red onion, peeled and finely diced
> 1 clove garlic, finely chopped
> 2 tablespoons homemade tomato sauce (see pages 98–99)
> 3 tablespoons olive oil and 1 tablespoon balsamic vinegar or lemon juice combined (for the dressing)
> pepper and salt
> 1 tablespoon chopped herbs of choice (basil, coriander, chives or spring onions)

1. Rinse the lentils after soaking, cover with water and bring to the boil. Simmer for 10–15 minutes until tender but not soft (avoid mush). Strain and rinse again.

2. Sauté the bacon, onion and garlic for a few minutes. Add cooked lentils and tomato sauce.

3. Put into a serving dish. Pour over dressing while the lentils are still warm.

4. Serve tepid, not cold, to enjoy all the flavours. Sprinkle with herbs of choice just before serving.

Carolyn's Caesar Salad
• ENOUGH FOR A LARGE SALAD

Not only is Carolyn a champion City to Surf participant but a champion Caesar Salad maker — not a leaf is ever left.

1 cos lettuce, leaves separated and washed
1 Lebanese cucumber, sliced
3 egg-shaped tomatoes, quartered
3 hard-boiled eggs, halved
1 ripe but firm avocado, sliced
4 rashers of bacon, chopped and fried until browning
8–10 anchovies (If they're very big you can cut them in half)
 (It's us and them when it comes to anchovies, but I say that a
 Caesar without them is an emasculated Caesar indeed)
12 or so fresh basil leaves

DRESSING
 ¼ cup olive oil
 ¼ cup balsamic vinegar

I. Into a wide salad dish or platter goes the cos lettuce to start, then the cucumber and tomatoes, the eggs artfully strewn here and there, the avocado similarly included, then the bacon sprinkled all over the top and the glistening prize of the anchovies left until last (if you're going to have them, don't hide them).

2. Toss in the basil leaves.

3. Dress with good olive oil and balsamic vinegar.

Roger's Summer Pudding
• SERVES 8–10

It looks stunning, like its maker, and tastes delicious.

500 g strawberries
300 g raspberries
300 g blackberries
250 g sugar
½ to ¾ cup water
1 loaf white sliced day-old bread (Don't use bread that is 'doughy')

1. Simmer the fruit, sugar and water until the fruit is tender and the sugar has dissolved.
2. Remove from heat and allow to cool.
3. Line two 600 ml pudding basins with slices of de-crusted bread.
4. Fill the basins with fruit mix, reserving the excess syrup.
5. Seal off the fruit mix with bread slices.
6. Cover the basins with saucers and store overnight in the fridge.

TO SERVE

Tip the pudding out onto a serving plate and use the reserved syrup to cover any areas of bread that are not already soaked in juice. Slice and serve with whipped cream and/or icecream.

Tim's Pavlova
• SERVES 6–8

Tim is a painter of still lifes. His voluptuous, sensual pictures inspire images of love and passion. No wonder he makes a pavlova to die for.

Here is his recipe in his own words.

This delicious dish was made by a clever chef who served it to and named it after a visiting European stage artiste.

She was either a very beautiful singer or dancer and her name was Jessy. There are two parts: the meringue base and the filling.

MERINGUE BASE
> 3 or 4 egg whites
> 1 cup and a bit of caster sugar
> 1 small teaspoon vanilla flavouring essence
> 1 pinch cornflour
> ½ teaspoon white vinegar

FILLING
> 1 cup fresh cream
> 1 teaspoon caster sugar
> ½ teaspoon vanilla flavouring essence
> 3 passionfruit
> 2 bananas
> enough strawberries

1. Very carefully separate the egg whites from the yolks so that absolutely no yolk gets mixed in.
2. Put the whites into a medium-sized bowl and beat them either with a whisk (the best) or an electric beater.
3. When the whites form stiff peaks, start adding the caster sugar a dessert spoon at a time, quite slowly . . . keep beating.

4. When the sugar is finished quickly add the cornflour, vanilla and vinegar and beat them in too.

5. Turn the oven on to slow (120°C).

6. Take a large flat tray and cover with foil carefully so that there are no wrinkles.

7. Using a bowl scraper make a nice cup shape on the tray with all the mixture. To do this, first scoop out about a third of the mix onto the tray and shape it into a round, flat circle, then add a dollop at a time to make the sides. (**WARNING:** Be careful as it's hard not to lick your fingers too much and make yourself sick.)

8. Gently put the finished masterpiece into the warm oven and leave for at least 1 hour – or even 2 – until it goes a nice pale brown. The longer you leave it, the stickier it gets in the middle.

9. After it's cooked, remove from the oven and let cool. Very gently peel off the foil. Lay it on a serving platter.

TO MAKE THE FILLING

This should not be done until it's nearly ready to eat. The base should be cooked and cool. In a bowl, whip the cream with the caster sugar and vanilla. Slice the bananas into the middle of the base and put the cream on top. Arrange the strawberry halves on top of the cream in a pretty pattern you must make up yourself. Then sprinkle the passionfruit on top of all this and then . . .

Wow! Yum! Yum!

HOW TO DEFEND YOUR PAVLOVA

First, line up your troops in a standard defensive pattern . . . and so on and so on.

Index